Ears & Emprise

Wild, then captive, now domestic.
By *Tess Zorba* and *Andrea Krebsbach*

Ears and Emprise *is a true story, a retrospective account of my ambitions to gentle a spirited wild-born burro at a boarding facility. Our journey was riddled with obstacles including an emotionally-demanding job dominating my waking hours and my cripplingly erroneous belief that my experience with horses had somehow prepared me to train a donkey.*

If you are interested in finding real pictures depicting our journey, follow belle_and_bray *on Instagram or like our* Belle & Bray *page on Facebook.*

Prologue

Six months into our journey, I was overwhelmed.

Overwhelmed by the progress that we had made, overwhelmed by the bravery that a fearful young animal had mustered in an environment where everything was both new and terrifying, overwhelmed by the grace that the animal had shown me when I made mistakes-

And the mistakes were numerous as I learned by trial and error, struggling to apply horse training techniques to a creature that was not a horse.

I was overwhelmed by the demands of an emotionally-draining career, overwhelmed by tight deadlines for graduate school assignments, overwhelmed by fatigue, overwhelmed by the lack of free time in my heavily scheduled weeks.

I leveraged my albeit-limited time off to the best of my ability to work with my newly-adopted burro. The first day that I was able to pick up one of her feet without any restraints or resistance, I was so proud of our success that I had the idea to start a journal of our landmark victories. I wanted to remember that incredible feeling of accomplishment. So, I went home after a short training session with my burro, immediately pulled out my monthly planner, and wrote "picked up Noel's feet without a rope for the first time" in the box for May 21, 2018. I vowed to make an effort to document the rest of our accomplishments in that planner. I thought it could even be exciting to compile those milestones into a book one day.

Flipping through the remaining pages of my 2018 planner, there are no other milestones documented. Instead, the days are filled with scribbles trying to organize the rest of my life into some semblance of a manageable plan. "Work 6:45 to 7:15" is scrawled across three or four days per week, in addition to work-related responsibilities such as "charge nurse," or "orient new LPN to the floor." The days that aren't overtaken by twelve-hour nursing shifts are dominated instead by graduate school assignments. "Write 10 pages for Nurse Leadership class," "complete discussion boards," and "sign up for next available courses," fill most of my days off work.

In between school and shifts at the hospital, I scheduled miscellaneous tasks such as dentist appointments, classes on Fort Carson to learn the responsibilities of volunteering as a Family Readiness Group leader for the unit my husband commanded, and reserving a few hours on some mornings to hike the Manitou Incline or go for a long run. I squeezed in time to train for a half marathon only because spending money on entry fees for races was my biggest motivating factor to stay in shape and run regularly.

I was busy. The barn was my sweet escape, both emotionally and geographically. Twenty miles north of my home and work, tucked back in the trees, I could breathe more freely at the barn. I had limited cell service, so I was able to put almost everything else on the back burner when I spent time with the animals.

With work and school demanding endless objective measurements of my success, setting black and white goals for my horse and burro companions was the last thing my tired brain wanted to do. Instead, I celebrated our victories during blissful moments of peace, then returned to my hectic life twenty miles south.

When the first anniversary of Noel's homecoming passed, it wasn't lost on me that she fulfilled achievements that even some animals born and raised in domesticity struggle to accomplish. She would hop onto an enclosed horse trailer with no fear, run to greet me in a wide, open field, and stand without a halter or rope for her hooves to be cleaned. On one occasion, she even accompanied her horse sister, Belle, on a trip to the veterinary clinic and stood more calmly in the loud, cramped quarters than sixteen-year-old, well-travelled Belle managed.

Yes, time and time again I was struck with a reminder that this was a journey deserving of documentation, but I hadn't taken the time to jot down more than a paragraph or two here and there about the outcomes of our daily sessions along the way. Most of my memories were vivid, though, so I thought, maybe, sometime in the distant future, a book about the sweet jennet who seemed to capture the attention and admiration of everyone who met her could still come to fruition. I could simply write it in retrospect everything that I recalled. I could even research her probable beginnings, with the limited information I had available about her past. After all, Noel had been born in the wild, then entered the government-managed wild horse and burro program before she became mine- surely I could find a paper trail detailing her beginnings.

The Army notified my husband that we would be moving in the summer of 2019, and I rejoiced, terminating my employment at the hospital that employed me as soon as the orders hit our inbox. Not only was there a lot to do to prepare for a cross-country move, but I had been desperately hoping for the chance to free up some of my time for several months. I couldn't justify giving up the lucrative federal position as long as we would still be living in Colorado, so military orders to relocate seemed like a gift from the universe. I was prepared to slash my already-minimal spending habits and leech off my savings in the name of free time, citing a need to mentally recharge and regroup.

I needed a few months off.

Having more time to sip hot coffee in the mornings and scroll through my phone, the realization dawned on me that, in fact, every step of Noel's journey from wild to gentled had been documented in far greater detail than a few words jotted in my planner would ever have captured. With over 12,000 photos stored in the gallery on my phone that I hadn't bothered to clear out in more than two years, her story unfolded with a flick of my thumb on the screen.

There she was, tense and unamused, on the end of a rope in Fairplay, Colorado, on the first morning in 2017 that Joe and I met an untamed soul named Zorba. There she stood, her fur covered in frost, on a morning that the temperature fell to zero degrees in Black Forest. And there- that photo is the first time I can see her brown eyes softening and her jaw unclenched in my presence. Another tap of my finger could unveil the exact date and time that the image was captured.

The excitement of my discovery set my fingertips on fire. My muse, this gallery of progress, inspired me to translate unfiltered cell phone images into her story- the tale of an uninhibited soul plucked involuntarily from her homeland who gracefully allowed herself to be transformed into a curious, still-wild-at-heart, domestic companion.

I had brought Noel home anticipating I'd use fifteen years of experience with horses to teach Noel all the things an equine in captivity needs to know. Instead, Noel taught me how foolish I was.

She didn't hesitate to show me time and time again that burros are not horses, nor do they think or react the same way. She taught me that it's imperative to find humor when things don't go according to plan. She taught me the difference between blind confidence and self-assuredness, as I doubted my abilities more than ever during the first few challenging months of attempting to train her, but refused to lose hope that we'd accomplish the ultimate goal of domesticity. Noel taught me how rewarding it can be to go for it, to dream big, and to take hold of your dreams.

Hopefully, her story will inspire others to do the same.

So, regardless of whether you're the person preparing to take a chance on a soul in need, or the person who enjoys watching from afar but knows you'll never embark on a journey like ours, or even if you're someone who already feels like you're in over your head with a project you underestimated.... Just take it.

Take the pictures. Take a risk on the dream that still gives you butterflies. Take the opportunity to quit the job you hate. Take a leap of faith into an endeavor without knowing what the outcome will be. Take a pay cut if it means taking your life back. Take time to relax. Take that insult as a joke. Take the trip. Take a piece of advice even when you're positive you don't need it. Take yourself seriously, but not without taking time to laugh. And, if it applies to you, take the chance on adopting someone who needs you, whether it's a human soul or an animal with paws, hooves, or feathers.

Take it.

You might find, like I did, that even when you're expecting to be the one imparting wisdom and bettering another spirit, you end up taking more than you give- and that both of you are better for it.

I. WILD

August 1, 2015
The Chemehuevi Reservation, California
One Day Wild

SEVEN O'CLOCK IN THE MORNING, and it was already hot.

Summer in the Chemehuevi region saw temperatures well over 100 degrees Fahrenheit on a daily basis. On the first day of August, the sun hung overhead for nearly fourteen hours, baking the plants, animals, and people living along the Colorado River south of the Mojave Preservation.

The salt-and-pepper jennet had been pacing back and forth through the sparsely-shrubbed landscape for a few hours. Instinctually, she knew it was almost time to lie down. Her udder had swelled, making travel more uncomfortable. She might have been pregnant for as long as fourteen months, or maybe as a few as eleven- there was no way to know, and the length of gestation in donkeys varies widely even among healthy pregnancies.

She found a patch of shade against a larger grove of sagebrush. Dropping first to her knees, the jennet lowered her swollen belly to the cool ground. Labor in donkeys is notoriously fast compared to other species, and within minutes, a small, dark muzzle resting on two wet, fingerlike angel hooves made its first appearance. Diving nose-first, the foal was deposited on the cool sand, sending a sun spider scattering away.

The foal's eyes were wide and bright immediately, nostrils flaring to break loose the mucous plugging its airway. Clumsily flicking the long ears atop its head, the foal remained perched on two wet, folded knees as its mother rose to her feet, licking the top of the foal's head first. The hot, dry desert air cured the soft tendrils of eponychium that had padded the foal's hooves inside the uterus, and, within moments, the foal's feet resembled normal donkey hooves.

Instinct drove the foal to unfold its legs, and after a thorough cleaning, it was standing precariously in the shade, its tiny hooves sinking into the cool sand. A few wobbly steps thrust the foal into the brilliant sun, drying the remnants of moisture clinging to parts of its fur.

Food.

The foal was hungry, and soon found its mother's engorged udder. Flicking its skinny tail happily in the sunlight, the foal began drinking. It would consume nearly two liters of nutritious colostrum by the time the sun set on the desert that same evening.

Shelter.

Glued to its mom's side, the foal was safe.

August 1, 2015
Clarksville, Tennessee
Full-time Nursing Assistant and Nursing Student

It's easy to be oblivious to the rest of the world when your own life is so chaotic.

At age twenty-six, I knew nothing about the plight of the wild burros in the West, nor would I have guessed that a little gray foal that had just hit the ground in California would have any bearing over my life in the future.

7:00 A.M. in southern California equated to 9:00 A.M. in Clarksville, Tennessee. Having just clocked out of an overnight shift at the local medical center working as a nursing assistant, I came home to an empty house, save for the dogs, called a tall glass of merlot both breakfast and dinner, and used a binder clip to secure the blackout curtains across the window so that I could get some sleep.

Working night shift left me in a chronic state of fatigue, and I drifted to sleep easily, blocking thoughts of my upcoming semester of nursing school from my mind. Just one more night shift, and I would be done with work for six entire days, on my way to Columbus, Georgia to visit Joe.

My husband had been stationed at Fort Campbell, Kentucky, when we got married. I moved from Indiana to the house he'd bought in Tennessee, just over the Kentucky state line, and started nursing school. Less than a month after I arrived, he deployed to Afghanistan, leaving me on my own with the dogs, Max and Audrey, for the first two semesters of nursing school. He redeployed home at the end of the year but less than two weeks later, moved to Fort Benning, Georgia on Army orders, separating us once again.

At least Fort Benning was a place I could visit.

I had secured work as a nursing assistant at the local medical center over the summer to gain some experience before graduating and becoming a Registered Nurse. I had opted for night shift because I was concerned that I'd be assigned a night shift capstone experience in the fall, and I wanted to prepare for the task of staying awake all night. It wasn't natural for me. Fast asleep by 10:00 P.M when given the chance, I required probably-unsafe amounts of caffeine to stay awake for the duration of my long shifts, and still struggled with getting enough sleep during the day to refuel my exhausted body.

The best part of twelve-hour shifts was only having to work three of them in a week to equate to full-time hours. I grouped six shifts together, and then enjoyed up to a week off at a time before having to start back over. Over the summer, I was using my extended breaks to spend some time further south.

We were due for military orders to move us to another state sometime around the same time as my graduation from nursing school in December of 2015. Just a few more months to persevere, and then we'd be packing up both the house in Tennessee and Joe's apartment in Georgia to move somewhere, together. Where, we weren't yet sure, but we were looking forward to spending more than a few days at a time under the same roof.

As fate would have it, we soon would receive orders to Fort Carson, Colorado. We didn't know at the time that we would make a home on the front range of the Rocky Mountains, where the snow had fallen over the duration of the long winter months and then spent all summer melting to feed the Colorado River. It was a source of water that flowed as far as southern California, providing hydration to a wild, nameless jennet, who gave birth in the early morning hours to a tiny foal that would one day join our family.

August 15, 2015
The Chemehuevi Reservation, California
Two Weeks Wild

Confusion.
Barely old enough to have learned what to do in the face of crisis, a tiny, two-week-old foal on spindly legs scrambled after its mother. The big, salt-and-pepper jennet was trotting with her head held high, moving faster than usual, pacing along the fence line.

The morning of her fifteenth day of life had started like any other. The little foal frolicked in the sun in the early morning light, staying close to its mother, but feeling comfortable in relatively close proximity to a handful of other burros. The foal watched its mother dig for water, pawing the sand using a front hoof. When no significant amount of fluid filled the basin, the salt-and-pepper jennet started migrating.

The foal had grown accustomed to spending a lot of time on its legs. The pair would walk significant distances, moving at a methodical but ground-covering pace, to graze on sparse bits of vegetation. They would walk in search of water, and walk to find safe places to lie down.

But they'd never started walking and found themselves unable to move any further.

With an immature brain perched between the long ears that the foal had finally figured out how to hold erect, the foal wasn't sure why they'd entered the pen. It didn't know that the sweet scent of alfalfa had wafted to its mother's nostrils, promising a delicious, nutrient-dense treat that was a far cry from the vegetation they typically nibbled as they strolled across the desert. A wide V-shaped enclosure had gently guided the burros into the pen, and the foal's mother indulged in a few mouthfuls of tender alfalfa shoots before a metal gate had clanged behind them.

The sudden noise startled the foal's mother off the alfalfa, and an anxiety-fueled lap around the pen had revealed no exit. The foal knew no differently, but it watched its mother search the perimeter once, then twice. The jennet lined her body up with one of the panels, then pushed hard with her haunches against the sand, scrambling for traction, attempting to push her way through the barrier. But the panels did not yield. The jennet lapped the pen again, searching, then made an attempt to dive, nose-first, underneath.

But the gap underneath was not big enough to permit an escape.

There was no exit.

The jennet came to a halt, hypervigilant, surveying their surroundings.

Constriction.

She noticed a human near the pen wearing a broad-rimmed hat. He was not an entirely new sight to the pair. Before the foal was born, the jennet often wandered into the outskirts of the nearby town, borrowing gulps of water from whatever source she could find or grazing on the richer vegetation cultivated by the two-legged population.

They stood now, face to face, with a single steel panel separating them. There was no way for the man to explain to the jennet that they meant no harm, nor that, ironically, the burro population's frequent ventures onto human-occupied terrain was actually the very reason they'd been baited into the pen.

Not understanding the new situation, the jennet remained wary and kept as much distance as possible. She stood between the man and her foal, protecting the skinny, young baby.

The man had a radio and a clipboard. He peered at the jennet and the foal, then spoke into the handheld radio. It was the first time the foal had been characterized.

She was a girl.

Clanging.

More noises began to approach the jennet and the filly as a truck and long stock trailer backed towards the pen. More two-legged people appeared, assisting the trailer into alignment with the pen. Accented by more sharp noises, the trailer door was opened, and they were supposed to go inside.

The closer any man got to the jennet, the more pressure she felt to move. Instinctually, the jennet moved away from pressure, and the filly followed suit.

She was young, but she was learning that when men got closer, the goal was to move away, as far as possible. In this scary new environment, it was survival.

On the trailer, the door closed behind them, leaving the jennet to again search for an escape, and again coming up empty.

Confusion. Constriction. Clanging.

It would become the new pattern of their lives for the foreseeable future.

Herds of burros tend to scatter when frightened. This instinct is part of what makes them more difficult to round up than their wild counterpart, the mustang. A helicopter can guide an entire herd of mustangs skillfully into a corral. When burros scatter, however, it is difficult to capture more than a couple animals at a time. The refusal of the burros to yield to their captors perpetuates the general idea that burros are stubborn animals. More accurately, however, their ability to thwart their captors is just an example of their smarts and athleticism.

Documents from the Chemehuevi burro roundup state that helicopters and horseback riders were not used in the operation, although some sources further explain that riders mounted on horseback do help encourage the burros to find their way towards the traps to expedite the process when there is a concern about animals become stressed and overheated. A two-week old foal certainly would have been at a bigger risk of succumbing to a stressful situation than an adult burro, and August in the Mojave Desert is not a welcoming environment.

The entire operation of rounding up burros and mustangs in the West is controversial. There are strong supporters on one side of the debate who believe that the animals should be left to roam free. Others argue that burros and mustangs are an invasive pest, not native to the Western landscape and that they should be eradicated. Still others waver in the middle, believing that it's okay for some wild horses and burros to live free in the West, but that the nuisance herds should be removed and remaining herds should be culled to control numbers.

I can understand a piece of each perspective. I do think that mustangs are an iconic symbol of the American West, and my emotional side feels strongly that it would be devastating to eradicate them. Yet, I also see stories of wild burros being hit by cars when they wander onto highways, and, living and working on Army installations, I have heard firsthand stories of brazen burros interfering with military operations in the deserts of California.

I choose to not waste too much time or energy dwelling on my stance on the issue as a whole. My singular opinion bears little weight, and I am not in a position to add political lobbying to my to-do list at this point.

What I do know is that there are close to 50,000 animals in government holding facilities, mostly untouched, with untapped potential.

One person can't change the world on her own.

But, one person, any person, has the ability to make the world for one animal change.

August 16, 2015
The Chemehuevi Reservation, California
One Day Captive

The line of burros snaked between a sea of corral panels. The little burro foal could feel other animals bumping into her on both sides. She still stayed glued to her mom, perhaps even more now than before. Her newborn hair was thin and she could feel the sun over the Mojave Desert baking onto her skin.

Inch by inch, she approached the front of the line. Her mom got there first, the little foal cowering behind her. She watched with wide brown eyes as her mom entered a narrow chute and a gate closed off all contact the little foal had. She brayed her panicked protests, but her voice was still little more than a squeak.

And then it was her turn. The sides of the chute closed in tight against her ribs, and she felt a cold pressure against the left side of her neck. She argued against it, her lips clenched into a rebellious scowl and her small gray ears pinned close to her neck.

It wasn't painful, but it was still happening against her will. Her mother had taught her to move away from pressure, but the squeeze chute made it impossible.

It was over in a matter of seconds. And just like that, the little foal had an identity, a series of symbols to represent government registration, her year of birth, and her individual identification number.

Abbreviated numerically, she was #0433.

It was the closest thing she'd have to a name for two more years.

Saturday, August 15, 2015
Columbus, Georgia
Senior Nursing Student

Leveraging more perks of night shift, I timed my nearly-seven-hour drives from Columbus, Georgia, to Clarksville, Tennessee so that I could leave when the sun started to set and drive all night. I could finish up a nap in the afternoon by the poolside at Joe's apartment complex, then pack up Max and Audrey and get onto US-280 before dark, arriving home in Clarksville with enough time to sleep through the daylight hours and wake up somewhat-rested for work by 7:00 P.M.

Driving four hundred miles in the dark can either be a very difficult life-or-death game of trying to keep your eyes open, or a completely entrancing experience, depending on the level of caffeine in the blood of the driver. I worked hard to sustain my status in the latter category, which allowed the luxury of long periods of deep reflection.

Living in the moment was, and is, a struggle for me. At the slightest opportunity to put my brain on autopilot, daydreams would take advantage and crowd all rational thought from my head. Driving was one of the best ways to distract me as I could methodically shift gears in my five-speed compact, subconsciously heeding traffic laws, remembering to glance periodically at the speedometer.

My last semester of nursing school would start on Monday. It didn't seem real that this car had been carrying me and my books under the community college archway for the past eighteen months. It felt like a small success just having survived the first three semesters of nursing school. Approaching this last term of classes felt both victorious and terrifying. I still felt that I had no idea how to care for patients.

I had decided to enter the nursing profession for a variety of reasons. I certainly had aspects of humanity on my mind- I liked being able to advocate for souls who could not do so for themselves. I also liked the idea of being part of a team of intelligent, educated professionals working together to change lives, and the hospital setting seemed like one of the most exciting places to do just that. As a health-conscious person with no significant medical record, I had rarely seen doctors, and the entire health care industry seemed a little exotic.

I broke into the medical industry during my first college career by taking night classes to earn an Emergency Medical Technician license. Working weekends on an ambulance, I had routinely picked patients up from hospitals, barely understanding half of the report that bedside nurses spit at me in between their dozens of other high-priority tasks. After a transport anywhere from across the street to across the state, I would then drop patients off in the more capable, educated hands of the physicians and nurses in emergency departments. It was exciting. I admired the professionals who were skilled enough to save lives when I could barely pronounce some of the patients' admitting diagnoses. It seemed fulfilling to apply years of schooling towards making a difference in the lives of people.

I'd initially entertained my passion for animals as a career, when I declared myself a pre-veterinary medicine major and studied Animal Sciences during my undergraduate years at Purdue University. I had thought it was the obvious choice when I was eighteen years old. I thought it was be gratifying to study ways to help animals and eventually base a career around my passion. But it wasn't at all what I expected.

I volunteered at the veterinary hospital on campus during the sophomore year of my undergraduate studies. During my oncology clinical rotation, however, I started to have second thoughts. I realized that I felt disappointingly obligated to show up every day. I disagreed with the plans of care for some of the cancer-positive animals on both a personal and moral level.

I remember specifically a seventeen-year-old cat that had been diagnosed with cancer. With the cat's quality of life significantly compromised by advanced cancer and coming to the end of a natural life span for a cat as it was, I felt that the cat would have been best off humanely euthanized to end its suffering. Instead, the cat underwent painful surgery and taxing chemotherapy. I remember asking if research done on these cancerous animals who were suffering through toxic treatments could eventually be applied to humans, but the veterinary staff told me that the type of cancer this cat was battling was specific to felines.

To me, it was a waste of suffering for the animal and a waste of resources to eek out a few more pain-riddled months of life. I struggled internally for a number of months before I realized that I wasn't going to find my passion in veterinary medicine, where I'd have to take an oath to keep animals alive at the owner's request even when my personal moral compass felt it was more humane to end the suffering.

I met with my academic advisor and changed the concentration of my major to Animal Production, a degree program that offered me more husbandry, nutrition, and behavior classes, the types of things I really wanted to learn.

But I still didn't find a passion.

In animal husbandry, I was required to pluck chickens for a grade, while the animals squawked and flapped in response to the pain we were inducing. I castrated a baby pig, my hands shaking as I sliced the scalpel though its unanesthetized scrotum and manually plucked its testicles from its body.

In nutrition classes, I was taught about the macros and the ingredients for diets that would fatten market sheep, hogs, and cattle to create the most profitable body composition. I could barely force myself to pay attention, instead spending most of those lectures daydreaming and doodling in my notebook. It didn't even begin to satisfy my passion for animals.

I sorted my way through so many classes in search of something fulfilling that I accumulated enough credits to graduate. I was even able to use that degree to secure a job in animal research, but knew immediately that my heart was not in it. So I spent nearly two years enduring a job I dreaded every morning to save up as much money as I could. Then, I quit, got married, moved to Tennessee, and started nursing school, all within the span of one month. I haven't squeezed that many milestones into a single month since.

Working now on the human side of health care, I can afford to make animals my hobby, prioritizing their care and planning the trajectory of their lives however I see fit. I love having the ability to make my animals happy and healthy, and I've found more passion in pampering my pets than in using animals in some way to bring home a paycheck.

The complete overtake of my daydreams was thwarted by Audrey's obnoxious panting in the backseat. Neither dog enjoyed long car rides, but at least Max cowered quietly under the seat so I could pretend he was napping for the duration of the drive home. Audrey perched in the center of the backseat, anxiously begging for the car to come to a halt.

"Four more hours, girl," I told her, and she whined her reply.

There was no way for me to know at the time that, while my world was opening up, on the other side of the country, the big world was closing for a little burro who'd barely gotten to enjoy her life unbridled.

II. CAPTIVE

August 15, 2016
Axtell Burro Facility, Axtell, Utah
One Year Captive

The barren countryside of Utah.

This was her normal.

She'd grown up enclosed, enmeshed in a nameless herd of other animals.

She could barely remember the time that, as a young foal, she could look at the horizon without seeing more metal panels encompassing her.

So this was it.

Life.

Sometimes throughout the day, there was fresh and plentiful hay available. At other times of day, she grazed for scraps on the barren earth. Sometimes, the sun rose. Other times, the sun set.

Repeat.

And repeat.

And repeat.

Until, quite unexpectedly, it wasn't her life anymore. Everything turned on its end once again when she was crowded once again onto a stock trailer.

Confusion. Constriction. Clanging.

It was happening again.

Winding roads, peaks and valleys, veers and lurches. She could only catch glimpses of the scenery through the panels of the stock trailer.

And then it stopped.

#0433 stepped off the trailer in a new place.

Colorado was no different to her than Utah. In fact, it was much the same.

Confusion. Constriction. Clanging.

A brief hiccup in her mundane routine, and then it started back over.

A new sea of panels in Cañon City, Colorado.

Home, for now, again.

#0433 likely had opportunities to leave the holding facility in Cañon City, but specific details of her individual story aren't recorded in any documents.

To be considered for a chance to leave the holding facility, there must first be interested parties who wanted to provide her a home. The types of people who have the resources and desire to bring home an untouched burro, though, are few and far between.

Some trainers join a program called TIP (Trainer Incentive Program), allowing them to incorporate gentling burros and mustangs into their business plan for a small profit.

"Not that one," she might have heard directed at her, if she was evaluated by a TIP trainer. Unresponsive to human interaction and very flighty when startled, she would have appeared much more difficult to train than more mature burros.

And nothing physical would have made her stand out. She didn't have unique spots or unusual coloring, wasn't excessively small or large, didn't have special markings. Her gray fur was the same monochrome color as most other burros, the Jerusalem cross draped across her shoulders in exactly the same way as most of the others.

She could have endured an auction, returning to the holding facility after receiving zero bids.

"Adopt a Living Legend," the dusty sign may have read, if she was there.

But audiences at such auctions are rarely packed. The bidders that do show up are looking for the same types of animals that TIP trainers want to find.

Calm, curious, or uniquely colored.

An animal that looks like it has potential.

Not a plain-appearing, nervous, unreceptive beast.

If an auction had been a part of her past, then she likely stood in a pen of a dozen or so other burros, tailed turned to the wind, huddled together for safety as a handful of potential adopters strolled by. Every once in awhile, someone with a crumpled paper number in his hand might stop at her pen and extend a hand. A couple of the more mature burros might have been curious enough to stretch their noses forward and sniff.

But #0433 likely held her ground safely in the back of the pack and averted her gaze from the wandering strangers.

She wanted to go back to the safety of the holding facility.

When it was her turn to run into the auction pen, she might have panicked as gates clanged behind her in the chute. She couldn't turn around or back up- the only direction to move would have been forward. She likely plunged, panicked, into the ring, instantly regretting her decision to move at all. Four tall walls would have surrounded her and the strangers with paper numbers who had stared at her all morning sat in the stands surrounding her on three sides, looking down at her with unamused expressions on their faces.

The speaker would have blared near her ears, causing her to lay them flat against her head. She might have darted around the perimeter of the ring, sizing up every crevice, determined to find one big enough to wiggle underneath. All to no avail. She may have turned her sights higher next- could she jump the panel?

If she couldn't find a corner low enough to clear, she may have tried using the brute strength of her yearling body to crash her way through. She could have thrown herself into the side of one metal panel, feeling the panel hit her back. She might have collapsed heavily onto her front legs, breathing hard as the speaker continued to blare.

The strangers in the stands would have continued to sit still. No paper numbers moved.

Finally, a loud metal gate would have clanged open again and she would have been ushered back to the corral. She probably trotted happily until she reached the safety of the herd.

She may have dived into the center of the drove and breathed heavily through her flared nostrils, her large ears collapsed to either side as if they were too heavy to hold upright any longer.

Burros tend to recover quickly from traumatizing ordeals. Back in the holding facility, she would have been relieved, and it wouldn't have taken her long to calm down.

At least her surroundings would have been familiar again.

She was imprisoned, and there she would stay because it was more comfortable than encountering the unknown.

This was life.

August 15, 2016
Colorado Springs, Colorado
Full-time Registered Nurse

    At 7:00 A.M., I was clocked in to begin another twelve-hour shift at the inpatient rehabilitation facility. I hadn't even had time to log into my mobile workstation before the call lights started flashing up and down the hall.

    It was a busy Monday because the rehab hospital always filled up on the weekends. The bigger hospitals in the area always wanted to pawn patients off to another facility before the weekend when all of the administrative employees were gone for two days. So, in the name of profit, the patients came here, to the second floor of the hospital where I was held captive for the day.

    Nine patients assigned to me. Each had multiple scheduled medications throughout the day, each needed to use the restroom multiple times throughout the day, and most experienced some level of pain requiring more medication before or after their therapy sessions. Three meals for each patient were served during my shift, so I'd help transport less mobile individuals to the dining hall or else properly position them in a bedside chair. Three of the patients required total care and were unable to walk at all, so I anticipated the use of bedpans, and I would have to find time to turn each person onto alternating sides every two hours to prevent pressure injuries.

It wasn't the worst job when I began, but new management had created a culture driven purely by profits with much less regard to patient safety. If I wasn't caring for at least seven patients, I was sent home unpaid. When a handful of nurses took their concerns to the new CEO, they were told it would simply be necessary to triage patient care for the foreseeable future, to just complete as many tasks as we had time to do in the span of our shifts and forget about the rest. Triage- appropriate for an emergency department, but not appropriate at an inpatient care facility.

I spent my lunch breaks scrolling through online job postings while I propped my throbbing feet on a chair in the empty break room. Every position that looked more interesting or less stressful required experience.

I was working on it. Six months of experience accumulated as of last week.

I was tired just thinking about working at this pace for another six months.

Maybe I should just start my Master's degree now to qualify for a job with more autonomy, I mused. I redirected the browser on my phone to search for online Master's in Nursing Science programs.

Ten minutes left of my lunch break before I had to return to my own prison, legally bound to the care of my patients until my relief arrived.

One year of experience was all I needed to qualify for a better job. That anniversary couldn't come soon enough.

February 1, 2017
Cañon City, Colorado
Six Months Captive

A new human outside the corral.

Burros never forget a face.

If she could understand English, she may have realized they were talking about her.

"Too timid," she'd heard before.

"Too fearful."

"No one wants that one."

No one, that is, until a single advocate stood up for her.

"I know a place she can go."

Those words were new.

Selected.

A new beginning, long overdue.

February 1, 2017
Colorado Springs, Colorado
Full-time Registered Nurse
Full-time Graduate Nursing Student

"Hi, I'm Andrea. I'm new here."

A new nurse, in a new hospital, introducing myself to new coworkers.

A new beginning, long overdue.

May 1, 2017
Fairplay, Colorado
One Year, Nine Months Captive
One Day Rescued

The time had come again.

Confusion. Constriction. Clanging.

Now, bumbling along in a rhythm she'd become all too familiar with, she swayed with the bumps and curves of the road, riding backwards in a breezy stock trailer. She was only sharing a trailer with one burro this time, another young jennet who stood a little taller than #0433.

The ride was long, but not as long as her move from Utah to Colorado. The air grew thinner, although large animals tend to suffer fewer side effects of the high altitude than humans. It was crisp, much chillier than the temperate valley she had left in Cañon City.

Whereas a horse has the ability to trap warm air between its winter coat and its skin to provide makeshift insulation, donkeys have no such mechanism, so #0433's hairs stood on end. She tucked her tail tightly and rounded her back and against the cold. She longed for the warm embrace of her mother's neck.

Where was her mother?

Unbeknownst to #0433, the trailer bounced past a humble wooden sign on its way to its final destination. *Far View Horse Rescue.*

A place unlike any she'd been.

Welcoming, cozy, friendly.

Her pen was smaller, but that meant fewer other souls trying to eat her hay.

The people were closer to her, and the attention they paid her was more one-on-one than any holding facility she'd experienced.

Kindness. Snacks. Smiles.

It was still unnerving for her to approach humans, but her burro instincts helped her quickly decide who she liked and who she'd rather avoid.

She liked a lot of the people here.

She was one of the lucky ones.

Rescued.

And just like that, #0433 had another identity.
They called her Zorba.

May 1, 2017
Colorado Springs, Colorado
Full-time Registered Nurse and Full-time Graduate Student

Beep-beep-beep.
5:00 P.M.

I reached over shut my alarm off, not that I had slept very well since noon. But it would be okay. One more twelve-hour shift, then I'd have three nights off in a row to recover.

Still in the honeymoon phase of believing my hopes for a better job had come to fruition, it wasn't as hard to drag myself to the new hospital as it had been at the old one.

I had settled into my new position on the medical/surgical ward quickly. I was motivated to prove that I was a valuable member of the team. I knew the names of all of my coworkers and most of the physicians, and the skills required to thrive in the more acute setting were becoming second nature.

I was relieved when I was asked to stay on night shift. I was happy to trade restful sleep a few days a week in order to associate with the more resourceful, down-to-earth nurses who had more freedom to care for patients without management breathing down their necks.

My days off became an alternating routine of sleep and researching topics for graduate school projects. A strong cup of coffee around 10:00 P.M. on my nights off was usually enough to fuel a bland regurgitation of facts and citations into APA research papers for graduate classes. Any free time left was dedicated to the barn. Our time together amounted to a few hours a week, but sitting with Belle in the silence was my getaway. Bliss.

Before I moved to Colorado, I had pictured the entirety of the West as endless ranches filled with cattle and horses. I was surprised to find most of the countryside vacant, save for whatever hardy plants found refuge in the hard, sandy soil and tolerated months without moisture. The land near Colorado Springs was a high desert, a far cry from the lush, green mountain sides I had imagined before our moving truck pulled up in front of our new home.

Living the Army life meant settling into a neighborhood close to post. Situated at the back of a subdivision, our yard was small enough that my late grandmother would have joked she could "cut it with a pair of scissors." So, when Belle had come out to Colorado to join me, she started a life at a boarding facility. It was a twenty mile drive from the house, but the commute was worth it because it was perfect. The facilities, the scenery, the management, and the fellow boarders were so ideal, I'm sure the experience will forever cast a shadow on any future boarding facility I use to house my animals.

Perfect.

Except one thing.

A very social animal, Belle bonded closely with her horsey neighbors, only to watch them leave when their training was complete, time and time again. Each time a friend left, she mourned their loss. She was becoming more withdrawn, and more anxious in situations that normally would not have fazed her.

Although no longer my priority, we sometimes went for short rides. Belle put herself through the paces under saddle, methodically jogging and loping on cue, but the spunk of her younger days was missing. We spent most of our riding time in the large outdoor arena, making circles in the sand, taking time to breath deeply in the midst of the tall pine trees. It was relaxingly routine, but the pep was missing from Belle's steps was noticeable. She was fourteen years old, so surely I couldn't expect to be greeted by the same sassy filly I had known a decade ago.

But was age the only factor?

Belle spent a lot of time alone in her house. Granted, even at baseline, Belle wasn't particularly outdoorsy for a horse. She was happiest on seventy-degree days, napping in the sun, and did tend to seek shelter at the slightest chance of rain or the upturn of the breeze. But it wasn't like her to stand inside all day alone even when the sun shone brightly.

An episode of colic raised the suspicion that an environmental stressor could be contributing to Belle's uneasiness. That colic scare was followed by another episode a few months afterward, and then another.

I had a fleeting thought about a solution, wondering if I could manipulate Belle's environment in a way that would facilitate her mental health.

"I think we need to get Belle a permanent friend," I said to Joe one day.

"Okay." He was surprisingly agreeable.

Really? I wondered, secretly wondering if he had considered all of the relevant factors such as the increased expense and time commitment, not to mention the increased difficulty of transporting two large animals across the country when we move, which we do every few years. But I didn't bring any of that up.

His agreeableness was a sign.

I ran with the idea of adopting a new animal, a Forever Friend, and began my search.

But what to get? What would make Belle happiest?

Off the bat, I knew the biggest criteria needed to be a female companion. If Belle had been born a human instead of a horse, she would have lived up to her name and been the belle of the ball at every social event, would have joined a sorority in college, and definitely would have looked forward to happy hour with her girlfriends after work on weeknights. Granted, she had gelding friends in the past, and rarely met a horse she didn't like, but always bonded more closely with fellow mares. So, *"be a girl"* went to the top of the list of criteria for her Forever Friend.

I'd heard of racehorses having companion miniatures horses and goats living in their stalls with them to help them stay calm when they travelled across the country for races, and both of those species technically could have been a valid option for my purposes. I briefly considered the idea of bringing home a goat to live with Belle. Briefly. I truly love all animals, but I love some more than others, and goats tend to fall close to the bottom of my list of favorites.

When I think of goats, one of the first memories that comes to mind is the time a goat ate the throat latch of my favorite bridle at a friend's barn, and then showed no remorse, bleating in my face when I tried to wrestle the rest of the bridle from his mouth, and headbutting me with his horns after I successfully retrieved it. The second image that comes to mind when I think about goats is their rectangular pupils that are a little bit creepy to me.

I scratched the idea of any type of goat as Belle's companion before I got too far down that rabbit hole.

Next, I considered a miniature horse to live with Belle. They're adorable, and they come in all shapes and sizes. They're portable, and *some* of them are easy to work with. The others, though, in my past experience, tend to act exorbitantly bossy and pushy just to prove that they're as tough as the bigger horses. But, if I was selective, I could probably find a mini that fit in with me and Belle.

So I added a long list of criteria that was necessary for the Forever Friend and started shopping. Firstly, because I worked long twelve- to thirteen-hour shifts at a hospital, there were, unfortunately, entire days that I couldn't visit the animals at the barn. For that reason, I wanted a mini that was already trained to lead on a halter and could have its feet easily and safely trimmed by a farrier so that my days off wouldn't be spent teaching a horse the basics.

Because I don't ride every day even when I do have time off work, Belle and I spent many afternoons hiking through the woods on foot, enjoying the beautiful Colorado landscape and soaking in the sunshine, so I wanted an animal that was friendly, sweet, and good-natured to accompany us on our mellow adventures.

Lastly, Belle was usually in the middle or bottom of the pecking order when she was turned loose with other horses, so I wanted a mini that was on the more submissive end of the spectrum so that it wouldn't boss Belle around or increase her stress level. The whole purpose of the Forever Friend was to make Belle happy and more comfortable in her surroundings while I was spending so much time away from the barn for work, and I needed to find her the right Friend to fulfill that goal.

Excited to begin my new project, I searched adoption sites, Craigslist, and Facebook groups... but I couldn't find anything that fit the bill. I was surprised to find only a handful of minis that were looking for new homes at the time, and the ones that were advertised just didn't fulfill enough of my criteria. I found one advertisement that read, "the vet estimates she's about 28-32 years old and she's not able to eat anything other than soaked beet pulp, but she still has a lot of good years left in her!"

Getting Belle a new friend with only a few years remaining on this planet, however, rather defeated my intent. I could only imagine the grief if she bonded with a friend for a few years, only to have it die shortly thereafter.

The next advertisement required four closely-bonded miniature horses to be adopted to the same home. I appreciated the efforts of the adopter to keep the bonded pals together, but I wasn't looking to give Belle an entire herd of new Forever Friends.

The ad after that was for a mini "with potential," code for "probably needs a lot of training," who required a "firm hand," code for "probably explosive and possibly aggressive sometimes."

The following ad was for a mini with multiple serious medical diagnoses that required multiple prescription medications to be administered three times a day.

Nothing for Belle.

I kept searching and exploring the topic of bringing a new mini home. During my research, I started to see some miniature donkeys lumped into topics discussing miniature horses. Many people think of them as being in the same category. Actually, I was one of those people at the time- they're both hooved equine, and one just has longer ears, right? But the pictures of miniature donkeys piqued my interest far more than the pictures of the little horses had.

Strikingly adorable.

I remember having a casual interest in donkeys over the years. A farm that neighbored the property where Belle lived for a short period of time in Indiana had a small herd of feral donkeys. I remember being intrigued by them, but was told that they were incredibly difficult to handle, and I was warned to stay away from them. Fifteen-year-old me obeyed.

Later, I remember regularly passing another farm that raised a small herd of miniature donkeys, and always slowing down to watch them play outside the window of my truck. They were so cute! They seemed exotic at the time- I didn't know anything about them. Who has a pet donkey, after all? The few people I knew personally who had interacted with donkeys at all had only negative things to say about how stubborn and mean they are.

Luckily, I'm really bad at listening to people when I've already decided to believe the opposite of what they're trying to tell me.

I'm an optimist to a fault in some aspects of my life, and my perceived ability to rehabilitate animals is one of those times. I grew up riding whichever horse a family friend would let me use for free during any given summer, or whatever horse I could find to ride in exchange for doing barn chores. That particular arrangement meant I saddled up a lot of animals that other people just didn't want to ride. I got bucked off sometimes, but there was never a time I didn't get back on. Instead, I read books and magazines, went to every horse training clinic that Indianapolis hosted, tried new techniques, tried again when I failed, and eventually overcame most of my training obstacles.

It wasn't just horses that I enjoyed helping and improving in my youth, either. In second grade, I brought home my friend's hamster because he had gotten loose in her house and had somehow lost a leg. The sight of his amputated limb was too gross for my friend to look at, and the poor hamster needed a new home with someone who didn't mind his new disability. Probably much to my parents' dismay, I was up to the challenge.

The next year, my parents agreed to adopt my first dog. I was ecstatic to get to the animal shelter and pick out my new best friend. When we got there, nine-year-old me was pretty disappointed that there was only one dog without a pending adoption, although, two decades later, adult me is impressed that there were so few homeless dogs in need of rescue at the local animal shelter. We adopted the only homeless dog in the county in 1997, a Lhasa Apso/schnauzer mix. "Scruffie" went on to complete ten years of dog shows in Hancock County 4-H with me. She brought home a trophy every year at the county level and twice at the state dog show. We even won a local award for being the first human-and-dog team to compete together for all ten years of my 4-H career. Most dogs are retired long before their tenth year of showing rolls around.

The same concept of rehabilitation-then-prosper continued when another friend reported she'd obtained two llamas who were a little more prone to kicking than she would have liked. Of course, they had a home with me. The kicking culprit, a giant male llama whose head stood two feet taller than mine, accompanied me to the county fair. Following the trend of my pets that had come before, we took first place in our class and went on to compete, and place, at the state fair.

I was a lifelong fan of the underdog, a devotee of the dark horse.

I was confident that, despite everything negative I'd heard in my life about donkeys, I could overcome a donkey's rumored stubbornness and shape a Forever Friend for Belle that would be both pleasant for me to spend time around and easy for people to handle.

I was up for the challenge.

I was positive.

Decidedly, I changed the focus of my search to "miniature donkeys" and pored over options.

Or, lack of options. There were even fewer choices for miniature donkeys within a hundred-mile radius of Belle's house than there were miniature horses.

Expanding the search to a two-hundred-mile radius didn't help.

Nor did a three-hundred-mile radius.

I finally found one option that I considered for a longer period of time than I'd considered any of the miniature horses. A farm about ninety minutes south of Belle's house bred and raised show-quality miniature donkeys. They were all spotted, which was the most adorable color pattern on a donkey, in my (former) opinion. They were trained, safe, and quiet. They were also $1200 each, although it wasn't the price tag that swayed me so much as the fact that I wasn't drawn to the show-quality aspect of the animals. It was completely unnecessary, and I realized that I really wanted to find a Forever Friend who needed a hand up in life, one who might not have many other options for a family.

Establishing where my priorities lied drew me to the local horse auctions. I went so far as to contact a few of the auction houses to ask how quickly I would need to remove animals from the premises if I won a bid on some poor soul. I didn't own a trailer at the time, and I didn't want to rent one every time I attended an auction. I was still planning on being pretty picky. I needed an animal who fit the criteria I'd established, because Belle was living at a boarding facility, and fully rehabilitating a rescued soul would have taken more resources than I had at my disposal.

I shopped the auctions for a couple of weeks, but nothing drew my attention, and my worries in regards to auction stock grew bigger. It's common for animals at auctions to be drugged, so it can be difficult to get a good idea of how an animal is going to behave at home based on the way an animal acts at an auction. Further, auction animals can be more prone to disease based on the filth they are exposed to on their journey, and I didn't have a great way to fully quarantine a potentially sickly, untrained Friend at a boarding facility. I really needed a donkey whose behaviors I could predict.

There's also a theory floating around the equine rescue community that buying underfed, neglected animals at auction simply causes the cycle of abuse and neglect of animals to persist. If horse dealers know that there's an easy, profitable outlet to dispose of their unwanted stock, then horse dealers, the bad ones, will continue to neglect and starve horses, mules, and donkeys in the name of profit. I understand this point of view, but I also, perhaps more strongly, relate to the idea that, while I don't have the capability to change an entire industry, *I can change the life of one animal* by rescuing it from a life of neglect and abuse that would otherwise terminate at a slaughterhouse in Mexico.

Someday, when I have forty acres of my own, I will be better equipped to change the lives of one slaughter-bound animal at a time.

In the meantime, there are still other ways to change the lives of animals without bidding on the saddest looking creature at an auction.

Beginning to feel discouraged in my search, I posted ads on Facebook groups and at the local Big R Farm and Feed Store. *"Seeking miniature donkey to befriend my lonely horse. Will provide a forever home."* But my posts and fliers attracted no prospects. I was feeling disheartened that there weren't any little donks seeking a forever home anywhere near Belle.

So I expanded my search even wider, and began contacting rescue organizations further away from Belle's barn.

I struck out at the first one.

The second one had several rehomeable donkeys that would have fit in quite nicely, but had a policy that they would never adopt a single donkey to a donkey-less household. The organization's viewpoint was that donkeys are happiest when they live with other donkeys, and I fully respect and understand that opinion. I do think that donkeys enjoy interacting with other donkeys, especially now that I know how incredibly unique donkeys are. I understand now that donkeys are not just long-eared horses. Everything, and I do mean *everything*, about donkeys differs from horses.

However, I also continue to support the concept that a donkey in need can befriend other species as well. When the options are a toss-up between never finding a forever home, or finding a forever home where the only companions are horses (or even other species!), I still feel that donkeys adapt and learn to enjoy the company of their horse friends, provided the horse friend also enjoys the company of the donkey. I have read multiple stories about donkeys bonding with emus, ducks, cows, and more, and they seem perfectly well-adjusted and happy. The biggest contingency is simply that donkeys need some kind, any kind, of friend to fall in love with. As long as they can bond with another living creature, they have all of the things they need to live a happy life.

I finally found a horse rescue in Fairplay, Colorado that had the same outlook as me, and would adopt a single donkey to an otherwise donkey-less household to live as a companion to a horse. I perused their website and found three donkeys available for adoption: Sage, Yoda, and Zorba. None of them were miniatures, and they weren't even on the small side as far as standard donkeys go. I visited the website to look at their pictures multiple times. I pulled the site up again, and then again. I even printed a hard copy of the adoption application, but I was hesitant to fill it out. Based on the descriptions on the website, none of the three donkeys at Far View Horse Rescue matched any of my criteria.

Meanwhile, over the months that I'd been searching for a Friend, Belle's outlook hadn't improved. She was sad, increasingly so. She continued to respond when I asked her to work, but it was obvious something was wrong. She lacked the playful spark she'd always had in years prior. She could often be found hiding out alone in her house with her head hanging low. When I asked her walk away from the barn alone, she became tense and anxious.

If it was any other animal, I might not have noticed the subtle behavior changes, or I might have attributed her flaws to needing a training tune-up. But I'd had Belle for fourteen years, and I knew her personality. This wasn't her.

I needed to help her.

It was unfair to ask her to live in misery when I was pretty confident that the "simple" addition of a Forever Friend would solve her problems.

So, on November 17, 2017, I pulled up the list of adoptable donkeys at Far View Horse Rescue again. Sage, Yoda, and Zorba. I ranked them.

Sage first, because she was the furthest along in her training.

Yoda next, for no reason other than she was a beautiful, unique brown color.

And Zorba came last, for no reason other than nothing unique stood out about her to me in her picture or online profile.

I contacted the rescue to find out if I could come meet the donkeys, and I quickly received a phone call from Far View's director.

"With Sage having just been adopted, I just want to make sure you understand that Yoda and Zorba still need A LOT of work. *A lot*. They have a *long* way to go. They were both wild burros, and they need a *lot* of training still," she stressed.

The emphasis was clear.

And I was completely unswayed.

Maybe it was the word "need" that piqued my interest. Maybe it was the fantastical idea of a formerly wild burro transitioning domesticated life. Either way, I was more convinced than ever that I needed to meet the two remaining donkeys. My list of criteria went out the window. Not trained? I don't care. Not even able to accept human touch…? Meh, we'll work on it. The idea of a wild-captured burro needing a home was too undeniably intriguing.

"That's okay," I remember saying casually. "I still want to meet them."

I was told that Zorba was the BLM (Bureau of Land Management) burro furthest along in her progress, and that she would probably be ready to go to a new home before Yoda.

Zorba.

My last choice on the initial ranking of the three animals that I'd made.

So I said, "that's fine," and immediately hung up to look at her picture again.

Zorba.

Her markings were undeniably plain. She was gray all over, with the standard Jerusalem cross across her back. I didn't really feel a connection to her picture. She had a hollow look in her eyes, completely disengaged. Nothing had stood out about her to me in her photo or her online description.

But she was the most ready for a new home, and I needed to gift Belle her Friend.

My next phone call was to my husband, who was out of state on a trip for work.

"So, there's a wild burro in Fairplay…"

November 20, 2017
Fairplay, Colorado
Two Years, Three Months Captive
Six Months Rescued

    Joe had done his best to sleep on a noisy bus on its way from the training range in Nevada to Fort Carson, Colorado. The bus pulled into the parking lot early, around 7:00 A.M. I picked him up on post and drove us immediately into the mountains towards Fairplay to meet the burro called Zorba.

    It was a two hour drive on a good day, and I'd gotten a phone call from the rescue shortly before we departed on the trip to warn me about the extreme winds on the northern plains of Colorado.

    "If you want to cancel, we completely understand. We have a high wind warning, and it's really bad up here."

    I considered, briefly, and felt a bit like the volunteers would prefer it, but my work schedule was far less than flexible, and Joe's schedule was even worse. The fact that we both had a day off at the same time to drive two hours into the mountains was remarkable. So I pushed onward.

    My very small Versa got great gas mileage and was paid off, so I had no qualms about driving it around town, but it was not the best-equipped vehicle to tackle Colorado's extreme weather, especially in the mountains. I was white-knuckled for most of the length of Highway 24. While sleep-deprived Joe dozed in the passenger seat, I did my best to keep the car between the lines and crossed my fingers that a gust of wind wouldn't pick the car up and flip it onto its side.

Tenaciously persisting forward, well below the speed limit even with the gas pedal pressed against the floor, we eventually arrived at the front gate of the Far View Horse Rescue. It was November in Colorado, and, at 10,000 feet altitude, the wind was bitingly cold on top of being sustained at over 50 mph.

We made our way towards the barns on foot, and the wave of a hand from the head rescuer pointed me towards Zorba. My gaze scanned the grounds, passed over a few equine nibbling hay, and landed on a gray burro standing just outside a three-sided run-in shelter amongst a herd of miniature horses.

Zorba's hair was long to protect against the cold, and upon her forehead sat the fluffiest bangs I'd seen adorn a donkey. It was clear that Zorba had seen us before we saw her. Her head was low, pointed in the direction of her hay feeder, but she had big, brown eyes that were quietly focused on the New Humans in her barnyard.

I didn't even take a picture of her the first time I laid my eyes on her. I was being open-minded, I convinced myself. I had coached myself that I wasn't in a position to just accept the first animal that was available. As a boarder and a modern-day gypsy who would move cross-country on a regular basis, I needed to find the right one. The right fit for Belle, the right fit for me, the right fit for our lifestyle.

But the argument was weak, even then, inside my head. It had been a long search just to find a potential Friend at all.

Joe and I approached Zorba and her miniature friends slowly, walking through the gate into their paddock with our eyes cast towards the ground to avoid intimidating her. It was obvious that she was skittish and shy. The mini horses living with Zorba, though, were extremely friendly, and eager to accept the cookies we had in our hands.

Zorba was much more cautious. She decidedly and committedly stepped away from our advances at first. Cookies were not an adequate reward for tolerating our presence.

By the time I had a rope in my hand, it had become my only goal to snap the clip onto Zorba's halter. The tunnel vision of Optimistic Rehabilitation mode had overtaken my consciousness, and I no longer felt the cold or the wind. I was focused on the present moment, working up to making contact. I was no longer evaluating Zorba, the potential Forever Friend. I was reading Zorba the Wild Burro's body language, interacting with her as submissively as possible to gain her trust. I meant her no harm, and convincing her that I was trustworthy was the only thought on my mind.

A few steps back and forth and some very hesitant, nervous energy from Zorba eventually culminated with the bull snap clicking satiably onto the O-ring dangling from the worn Nylon halter on her face.

Success.

I gave her a minute to adjust to the idea of the rope connecting her face to my hand. Zorba's tall ears were focused on me, her body still tense, but her big brown eyes soft. She was reading me. She just wanted to know what she was getting into by agreeing to accept the advances of my rope onto her halter.

My presence of mind refocused again, briefly, on the task at hand, and I stood up to assess Zorba's training status on a lead. I tried to remember the criteria I'd carried in my head for all the months that I'd been searching for the Forever Friend, but they wouldn't come to me. So we just walked. Well, we tried to walk.

Applying a small amount of tension on the lead caused Zorba to stiffen. She didn't like the concept of me applying pressure to her head to tell her to make a move. So, when I persisted with the pressure I was applying via the rope in my hand, she eventually reacted negatively, throwing the weight of her body in the opposite direction in an attempt to escape from me.

After a few, or, perhaps, many, attempts to guide Zorba and instead enduring her dragging me around the paddock, she finally took a step in the direction that I was asking her to walk. And that was it. A positive note, and a good reason to end our session. We put her back in her paddock with her miniature friends, and she walked away from us.

Calmly.

Hyper-aware of the positive, I noted specifically that she walked calmly away from us.

We drove away from Far View that afternoon, fighting again against the extreme wind, and I asked Joe what he thought about Zorba, trying to convince myself that I was still on the fence, trying to remind myself that I had set criteria for the Friend we were seeking for very valid reasons. I tried to ignore the uprising of my internal Optimistic Rehabilitator, but it was to no avail.

"She's cute. Let's do it," Joe said sleepily.

It was all the affirmation I needed.

Zorba's perspective on the same day was different.

Bracing against the cold each time the wind gusted, Zorba's focus early that morning was on the generous mountain of hay in front of her and her miniature roommates. They all munched quietly, chewing methodically, and it was a good morning. Zorba felt safe with the little horses, but she still kept her guard up almost constantly. Her strong survival instincts were the reason she'd been able to endure being weaned from her mother in a government holding facility without appearing any worse for the wear, and then enduring two long, interstate transports where she'd left friends behind each time.

	From her pen at the rescue, Zorba could barely see her friend Yoda, the big brown burro who had made the trip from Cañon City, Colorado, to Fairplay with her. They'd been separated shortly after arrival to prepare them for finding new homes, but Zorba didn't know that. All she understood was that she'd lost another friend that she'd met along her journey of life, and that she had to start over making acquaintances with her new crowd of miniature roommates. Zorba still brayed to her friend occasionally, and was comforted when a loud return bray echoed through the barnyard.

	It was windy, but the aluminum-sided house shielded Zorba from the worst of the gusts. Her hair was long, but she still wasn't completely accustomed to the frigid Colorado mountain air. Zorba was standing on ground two miles higher in elevation than the hot, sandy terrain in southern California where she was born just a little more than two years prior.

	The sight of two people walking down the driveway caught Zorba's attention. New People. She stopped chewing and backed a few steps into the safety of the run-in. She stood still, her head low and relaxed but her tall ears alert and fixated on the new visitors.

She knew she'd never met them before. The people were still far away, and, standing upwind, she couldn't smell them yet. But her eyesight was incredibly sharp, and her burro brain was incapable of forgetting. The New Humans walked with their heads ducked against the wind, stopping to talk to one of the rescuers who Zorba had gotten to know over the past few months. Yes, she had definitely never met them before.

Zorba watched the rescuer point at her, and then saw the New Humans follow the direction of her hand and let their gaze land upon the run-in where Zorba stood, their eyes taking a moment to adjust to the shadowed shelter standing against the glaring Colorado sun. Zorba still didn't move. She let them look at her, but she didn't interact. She kept her walls up, waiting for their attention to fall towards some other creature. It worked. The humans walked away, briefly, into the shelter of another barn.

Zorba stared after their absence for another moment, then relaxed just enough to step towards the hay feeder and take another bite.

She startled back to attention when the New Humans approached the gate leading into her pen and creaked it open. Rounding her rump and tucking her tail tightly against her legs, Zorba maintained every inch of her focus on the humans.

They were too close for comfort now, although they didn't walk towards her right away. Zorba stood several yards from the New Humans and watched them approach each of her mini roommates, smuggling cookies into their muzzles. The minis seemed relaxed and comfortable with their presence. But Zorba knew better.

While Zorba had enjoyed only positive human interaction during her time at the rescue, she'd also endured her fair share of questionable human contact during the first parts of her life. New Humans had been responsible for freeze branding the first name she'd ever had into her neck, when she became #0433. New Humans had been there when she'd been vaccinated and felt the hot sting of the needle plunge into her neck. New Humans were responsible for squeezing the clanging metal chute tightly around her, tipping her onto her side, and trimming her hooves at the government holding facility. Every time something scary had happened to her, it was New Humans who did it.

The minis happily finished the last crumbs of the cookies they'd been gifted, and Zorba could sense that she was up next. She walked away from the New Humans without blinking, her eyes staring at them from underneath her fluffy bangs. When they walked south, she beelined north. When they calmly diverted their route back towards the nervous donkey, she hustled in the opposite direction again.

She wasn't terrified, not the way she felt around some humans. She could sense that they were not aggressive. It still was safest, though, for her to stay away. So, back and forth they went.

The girl human was persistent, and Zorba focused on reading her intentions. She was submissive, her eyes never making contact with Zorba's, her movements slow and purposeful. She smelled like the pocketsful of cookies she carried with her. She had a calm, positive energy, and took regular breaks to give the mini horses some attention. Zorba would have been satisfied if all of the human's energy was focused on the minis.

Zorba eventually found herself poised in the run-in with an easy exit route available in front of her, and closely watched the girl human walk slowly towards Zorba's right shoulder. Zorba paused this time, waiting to see how the girl human would escalate. What was about to happen?

The girl human crouched, and Zorba allowed it. She kept all of her muscles tensed, ready to take off if she needed to run for her life.

An outstretched arm with a rope grasped in its hands moved slowly towards her chin. The girl human stayed relaxed, not speaking, not moving very quickly, her eyes focused on the ground. The rope grew closer, a sight Zorba had seen before. It had always been her favorite rescuer who sat with her during the day and told her stories, never this new girl human. But it didn't feel like an immediate threat to her life, so Zorba stayed still.

The familiar click of the snap broke the silence, and the girl human seemed satisfied. She still didn't move, though, and Zorba sized her up. She was short, appearing shorter still while she was crouched on the frozen ground. Her wild hair frizzled around her cold, flushed face but her eyes remained warm and soft. The girl human seemed to light up every time a mini approached her to kiss her cheek with its soft muzzle. Zorba wondered if the girl human knew that the mini horses were only interested in her because of the cookies in her pocket.

Over the next several minutes, the girl human slowly escalated the scale of her movements, and Zorba was less than impressed. When girl human tightened the slack in the rope, Zorba had to let her know that she wasn't some creature that could be easily bossed around like one of her mini horse roommates. Zorba plowed in the opposite direction each time, taking the girl human by surprise as she stumbled to keep her balance. Zorba dragged the girl human down the fence line in an attempt to get free, but, much to her dismay, the girl human held onto the end of the rope, doing her best to dig her heels into the frozen ground and stop the determined burro from getting free.

Zorba was at an impasse. She'd sized the girl human up, and knew that she was at least three hundred fifty pounds heavier than her. She'd thrown her entire body weight against the rope yet she was still the captive of the person at the other end. What else could she try to make this girl stop?

The girl human again picked up the slack in the rope and pulled gently against Zorba's halter. Zorba contemplated the sensation of pressure on her face for a moment, operating on burro time, not to be rushed. Her only goal was to make the annoying pressure stop, *and to survive*. She had tried pulling against the pressure half a dozen times, each occurrence resulting in increased pressure on her soft face. This time, she tried something new and gave into the pressure. Zorba took a tiny step towards the girl human to relieve the upsetting pulling sensation.

Amazingly, the pressure stopped. The slack returned to the rope, and the girl human turned slightly away. A release in pressure, both physically and emotionally. Zorba breathed out a little more deeply than she had in the minutes prior. It worked.

Zorba had won.

The girl human had pulled on her face, and all Zorba had to do was take a small step forward to make the girl stop. She had successfully trained the girl human to stop annoying her.

Zorba was allowed to go back to her pen after the tiny step she'd offered, and she was quite content leaving the New Humans behind at the gate to rejoin her small herd of minis and munch on more hay.

The New Humans again turned their faces away from the wind and started back on their journey down the driveway. The girl human gave Zorba one last glance before walking out of sight, her hands shoved into her newly-cookieless pockets, exchanging some inaudible words with the other human walking down the driveway. Zorba maintained an eye on them until they were out of sight, then relaxed a little more into the solitude of her mini herd.

She preferred the company of other equine, and she didn't like change, but she committed the girl human's face to her memory. Zorba wondered if she would see those New Humans again.

III. DOMESTIC

January 3, 2018
Black Forest, Colorado
Two Years, Five Months Captive
Eight Months Rescued
One Day Home

    From the top of the hill, I could see the truck and trailer steering towards our drive.

    She was here.

    Home.

    Belle's Forever Friend.

    Clanging, constriction, confusion, and then the trailer door opened. Bold and confident, Zorba made her debut as Noel, stepping onto the dirt and looking around.

    "She's incredibly calm," a group of us remarked, impressed that there wasn't a tantrum or any sign of nervousness. Noel stood in the center of the pen with a hind foot cocked, surveying the new environment that she didn't yet know was hers.

    I didn't know at the time that the unprecedented level of restraint and composure was less of a sign of complacency on Noel's behalf, and more of a sign of analytical deftness. She wasn't yet sure what the threats would be, so she laid extremely low, straightforwardly not bringing any attention to her until she'd completed a thorough assessment of the new situation she had involuntarily entered.

    At the time, to a new burro owner, I was simply relieved at Noel's placidity. She didn't even seem nervous to be in a new environment, surrounded by horses who were looking at her as if she was an alien. She wasn't pacing, braying, or pawing. She just stood, calmly, quietly, taking it all in.

I would come to learn that the quieter a burro is in a situation that should be inducing some anxiety, the more likely it is that she is plotting something diabolical.

But I had no idea.

I sat quietly in the pen for a few hours, not wanting to make Noel feel uncomfortable, but also wanting to be close by to make sure she continued to feel safe and calm. At some point during the afternoon, Belle was reintroduced to her pen to meet Noel for the first time.

The girls more or less ignored one another.

Anticlimactic, I thought.

Until the feed truck rolled around and it was time for Belle's dinner.

Enthusiastic about receiving her dinner, Belle used body language to make sure her new roommate was fully aware that they weren't yet in a place where sharing hay was an option. I was hovering nearby for the duration of dinnertime as Belle scooped mouthfuls of grain from her rubber pan into her mouth. Belle's halter was still on, and I was within a few arm lengths of her, but I didn't move fast enough to stop Belle from pinning her ears flat against her head and making a lunging step towards Noel to exhibit her possession over her dinner.

It wasn't an over-the-top aggressive reaction, and it wasn't anything outside of the norm as far as how horses interact with new additions to their herd. It happened in a fraction of a second, so quickly that I missed most of the event unfolding. But the change in Belle's body language from complacent to defensive of food was all it took to trigger Noel to use the exit strategy that she'd evidently been sizing up all afternoon.

With nostrils flared, her nose and two front hooves found their way between the lowest strand of impenetrable cable fencing and the ground- a gap of no more than eighteen inches. Then, with the determined might that only a wild burro on a mission can muster, one strong push with her hindquarters propelled her five-hundred-pound body under the fence, and she was gone.

What...

What just happened.

Tunnel vision closed in around my consciousness and it was as if my neurons were encased in a thick sludge of molasses, refusing to connect the dots and process the reality that my brand-new pet burro had just exited captivity and re-entered the wild.

I may as well have been watching a movie on a screen that kept flashing in and out of focus. I wasn't sure what had happened in the moments prior, so it was impossible to predict what was about to happen, no matter how hard I willed myself to concentrate.

"Up there!" and I was immediately thankful that other boarders were still out at the barn at dusk, ready and willing to help in the way that only the equine community draws together when large animals don't react according to plan. I followed the direction they pointed, my head turning slowly because it weighed fifty pounds more than usual, and saw the silhouette of a burro at the crest of the hill overlooking the barn, head high in the air, ears up, chest puffed out.

She looked down at us, briefly.

Then she was gone.

Again.

It was impossible to look objectively at the situation in the moment without feeling panic reverberating through every fiber of my body. I listened to my heartbeat in my ears as I pondered how to solve the dilemma I'd suddenly and unexpectedly encountered. Looking back, I'm positive that the adrenaline-fueled pounding in my head was probably the only thing masking the opening chords of The Fray's "Over My Head" beginning to tinkle softly in the background.

It would become the theme song for my first month of wild burro ownership.

I'm aware that it could be insightful, helpful, and possibly even educational to share the Great Escape and (spoiler) subsequent capture in greater detail to help any aspiring burro adopter who finds themselves in the same quandary solve the dilemma. I wish I could. But the details aren't there to share. I still have little more than a vague recollection of the events that unfolded over the subsequent few hours- or was it that long? It could have been over in thirty or forty minutes, I'm not sure. The timeline sits lazily as a dark, shapeless blob of a memory in the back of my mind, and no aspect of the escape nor the capture are depicted in any photos from that night. Photos were the last thing on my mind.

I'm forever grateful to the people who immediately jumped in to help, because I'm not sure that my stunned mind could have convinced my frozen body to take action so quickly without their prompting.

Camouflage.

It was the first realization that hit me. It was shockingly apparent how the wild burro population managed to hide out in the desert setting so expertly. It required a great deal of squinting and concentrating to make out the shape of the burro against the sandy backdrop of the sprawling ranch.

It was all hands on deck, but I couldn't make a list of people to thank even if I wanted to. My memory has a way of clouding around events that caused me distress so I don't have to endure the recollection.

Kindhearted people helped me track her down, still within the confines of the perimeter fencing. With a new awareness that the large animal could slither through an opening that appeared far too small for her mass with mouse-like capability, though, I knew the perimeter fencing was far from donkey-tight.

Trucks joined in on the chase, and when we found Noel pigeonholed into a long corridor of gates with only one exit, the vehicles blocked the escape route, giving us a chance to capture the truant creature.

A rodeo ensued. She wasn't interested in being captured, and she had the energy and strength to thwart every attempt we made.

When I was in high school, my family had fenced in a large portion of land at my grandmother's house and brought home a relatively large herd of llamas to do the mowing so that my eighty-year-old grandmother didn't have to climb aboard the riding lawn mower twice a week. Those antisocial llamas had trained me how to approach and subdue an animal that's not interested in having a halter attached to its head. Llamas, however, weigh in at just a couple hundred pounds, easily less than half the weight of the stout burro before me, and they have swan-like necks that are easier to wrap arms around.

I remember trying the same technique on my burro during the Great Escape.

I remember quickly learning that it doesn't work on wild burros.

Whatever sequence of events continued to ensue with the overwhelming help of the barn community eventually culminated in confining Noel in a cattle chute, allowing a rope to be attached.

With two ropes snapped onto either side of the halter, one hopeful human hanging onto each one, and a willing and good-natured pony leading the way, we got Noel back to the safety of the barnyard and tucked her into her own pen, a corral with steel panels on each side that would be more resistant to an attempt to squeeze through small gaps.

Every gate, usually swung wide open in a welcoming gape, was battened tightly closed. Maybe, we calculated, even if she escaped from the round pen, she'd be stymied by the next gate, or the next.

Only a few brave brain cells in the back of my head admitted that if the crafty, strong-willed animal in the round pen managed to find her way out, one more measly gate would likely do little to foil the rest of her escape.

Depleted. Driving home in the dark, shifting predictably from first gear, to second, to third, fourth, fifth, neutral, starting back over at each stoplight. The green lights were in my favor, one of the first strokes of good luck I got on the third day of the new year. I couldn't even formulate a complete sentence inside my own head.

I was tired.

"How'd it go?" Joe greeted me at the house.

"I think I got in over my head with this one."

January 4, 2018
Black Forest, Colorado
Two Years, Five Months Captive
Eight Months Rescued
Two Days Home

My stomach growled.

Had I even eaten dinner the night prior?

I didn't remember being hungry last night.

The sun was just rising over the eastern plains on my drive back to the barn, casting a pinkish glow across everything in its path and illuminating the snow-covered cap of Pike's Peak in the distance. I made a pit stop at a gas station for coffee and a banana. I hadn't slept much overnight, mostly due to worrying whether I would still have a burro by the time I awoke.

Mine was the first car to arrive at the barn. I strained my eyes, squinting to see whether Noel was still enclosed in the pen. Camouflage, I reminded myself, preparing myself to refrain from panicking if I didn't see her. But, there she was, focused on grazing across the short plant shoots shriveled in the crisp January air.

Relieved, I made my way to the pen with my breakfast in tow, overturning a plastic bucket to create a seat in the center of the corral. I sipped my first taste of coffee, appreciating the warm hug of caffeine.

"Good morning."

Noel watched me warily from the far side of the pen.

I removed my gloves to unpeel the banana, talking to her as I did so.

"I'm sorry yesterday was so stressful for you. For both of us."

She hadn't moved a muscle.

"I might have underestimated you." I took a bite of the banana, and she cocked her head slightly, her nostrils flaring.

I had her attention.

"I'll be honest with you. Last night, when I got home, I was pretty sure I was going to have to make a difficult phone call today and return you to the rescue."

Whiskers quivered.

"But I don't want to get discouraged too quickly. One day is not enough time to decide that this isn't going to work out. So, instead of sleeping last night, I decided that, for this entire month, we should just be. Just exist. We'll take it easy on ourselves. I won't worry about your progress or how much we have to learn. Let's just survive this one month, and then, in February, we take a step back and make sure this is going to work out."

She was creeping closer to me, her ears standing tall atop her head. It was almost as if she was understanding the words I was saying. I took another bite, and she stretched towards me, tiptoeing closer, quietly.

"Whatever you need this month, consider it yours. I'll throw whatever resources I have available into making this month comfortable. Into making it work for us. We probably need to secure a more permanent house for you, something escape-proof."

She was closer still.

It was the first time she had approached me with so much confidence and curiosity. It was surprising that she was so trusting after the Great Escape only twelve hours earlier.

She was within an arm's length of me and slowly shifting even closer, but I didn't reach out to touch her. I didn't turn my head to look at her. I let her explore, sniffing and eyeballing me. Then, satisfied with her safety assessment of the situation, she bent her head down-

And took a big bite of the half-eaten banana in my hand.

"Hey!" I laughed. Her lips had left sediment and sand clinging to the rest of my breakfast. She chewed, still looking at me, unapologetic, then tipped her head to the side again. This time, I reached towards her, offering the rest of the banana.

Noel stretched forward, but went a step beyond just taking another bite. Opening her mouth wide, she grabbed the banana peel in her mouth and yanked the entire piece of fruit from my hand, dropping it onto the ground a safer distance from me. It only took a few minutes for her to finish her treat, peel and all.

"Okay," I shrugged, taking another big drink from my Styrofoam cup before the burro decided she wanted to steal my coffee, too. "You win. I'll bring breakfast for the both of us next time."

It was our first conversation, far less one-sided than it probably would have appeared to anyone eavesdropping. I may have been the only party using words, but Noel was listening, and understood my tone and intent, if nothing else. She responded in a way that, I would come to find, only a burro can respond- more dramatically than I anticipated, and with a one-of-a-kind sense of humor, making me laugh when I least expected to find myself in good spirits.

Little did I know at the time that Noel would spend the next year keeping me on my toes, helping me learn and grow, while she navigated her new life. She would paradoxically take the big things in stride even when I expected an explosive reaction, and overreact in a dramatic fashion to the little things that I didn't expect would elicit a response at all.

It would have been handy if she came with a manual.

January 7, 2018
Black Forest, Colorado
Two Years, Five Months Captive
Eight Months Rescued
Four Days Home

What is money, anyway, I comforted myself, avoiding eye contact with the screen on the cash register as I handed my credit card over the counter. *Just a series of numbers that appear on my phone when I log into my bank account. Who needs it.*

I was the first person in line at the farm supply store on a Saturday morning. Being an early bird was becoming my new trend, something not usually associated with a night shift worker. My shiny new roll of galvanized cattle fencing, now paid for, was awaiting my pickup in the side lot, and the next obstacle I had to overcome was the stigma of asking the employees to load it into the backseat of my tiny car rather than the bed of a pickup that they were likely expecting.

"Ma'am... are you sure?" The two men in red vests peered into the backseat of my car, looked at each other, then looked back at me.

"Oh, yes," I said, feigning confidence. "I'm sure it will fit."

The look of doubt never erased itself from their faces, but the employees played along, squeezing 350 feet of cattle fencing into the backseat of my Versa with barely enough room to slam the doors closed.

It looked so ridiculous, I half-expected them to take a picture.

"And you're sure you have people to help you offload this when you get back home?"

"Of course," I lied. "It would have been nice if they were able to be here to help pick it up, but that's just the way it goes." I shrugged lightheartedly, nervously wondering how much the enormous roll of fencing weighed as I climbed into my driver's seat. I had a thirty-minute drive across town to come up with a plan for managing the roll of fencing on my own.

It started to sink in how much easier it would have been to wait for both my husband and his truck, but they were both were tied up for the day on Fort Carson, and I couldn't wait. I just couldn't. Patience had completely eluded me, and I wanted to start this project *now*.

Across town, I steered my little car through the barnyard, parking as close to Belle's pen as possible. My goal was to secure the cattle fencing to the existing foundation of steel poles and cables, eliminating any gaps that could be misconstrued as an exit by the crafty burro now in my care.

I wonder how hard it is to get a sponsorship for promoting the versatile use of Nissan's cheapest entry-level sedan, I thought, opening the car door and again becoming a little overwhelmed by the mass of metal I needed to wrestle into place.

The hideous-but-handy little car had even survived a journey through Monument Valley in Utah last summer, when Joe and I decided to drive closer to the iconic rock formations without realizing that we were embarking upon a rugged path intended only for four wheel drive vehicles. We made it through the entirety of Monument Valley in the Versa without losing a tire, even surviving a nerve-wracking climb up steep terrain with the gas pedal pressed against the floor in second gear and still losing speed and traction with every yard we climbed. Now functioning as a farm vehicle hauling heavy duty supplies, I was impressed with how much I'd been able to persuade my car to do, and enjoyed forty-four miles to the gallon and zero car payments along the way.

It was good I'd saved money on my car so I could spend it all on my new long-eared pet.

Taking a deep breath and donning a pair of gloves, I started on my first task: removing the roll of fencing from the car.

I tried several ways to get a solid grasp on the fencing, leveraging my legs against the weight of the roll, pulling hard, first in this direction, then that way.

Is it alive? It's fighting back against me! I thought in desperation, watching the fencing barely shift an inch at a time.

My workout built up enough heat even on a cold January day to doff my coat by the time the fencing was nearly free from its nest in my backseat. A final tug sent the bottom of the roll cascading down the passenger door of my car and onto the sand, leaving a healthy scratch in the plastic interior, and I groaned. Just another toll it was necessary for me to pay in the process of trying to create a safe home for my newest addition.

It would have been unfair to give her anything less than every possible chance to assimilate. Failing to set Noel up for success in her transition to domesticity would ensure a shortcoming. So, I'd predetermined that I'd provide all the resources she needed, and premedicate myself with a glass of wine before checking my credit card statement at the end of the month.

I was disappointed to discover that the wrestling match to get the roll of fencing out of the car was only the first small step in what was beginning to feel like an insurmountable task. Panting as I continued to make an inch of progress at a time, my arms, shoulders, and back were screaming by the time the roll of fencing was sitting in the correct spot for me to begin unrolling it. I allowed myself a drink of water, but didn't want to waste any more than a few minutes of daylight before proceeding.

All of these burros and mustangs sitting, unwanted, in holding pens across the West- people must not realize that bringing home a wild animal is a nearly-guaranteed weight loss and fitness program. *The sales pitches would write themselves,* I mused, fighting to force the fencing into place. Not only would monumental projects like dragging fencing around in the sand burn more calories than an hour at the gym, but they also eliminated any free time to eat meals, and required any extra money that could have once been spent on cupcakes. *And you can feed a burro or mustang for just about triple the price of monthly membership at an expensive fitness center.*

    I'd have to research who I could pitch my idea too, when I had free time again. But by the end of a day stringing the fencing into place a foot at a time, my forearms were scratched and bleeding from brushing against broken wires, and my muscles were too tired to even lift my wire cutters off the ground anymore.

    I wasn't sure I had the energy to drive home, let alone pitch any kind of marketing campaign.

    Noel watched the ridiculous scene unfold from the safety of her secure pen across the aisle.

    Quiet, unmoving, she soaked in as much of her new environment as possible.

    She saw the now-familiar human wrestling with an inanimate object, struggling under its weight, dragging it around the pen where the bully of a mare lived, the one who had chased her under the fence four days ago.

The human spent hours with the big block of silver lattice, sometimes pausing long enough to yelp, "ouch," rolling up a sleeve to survey the damage, and then shaking her arms. The bully mare stood idly by. The mare seemed lazy. Or, maybe, sad.

The human had caused her no harm, but Noel was wary. The cycle that had followed her through every transition in her life had begun again. Confusion. Confinement. Clanging. And now this human was fighting with some type of object that wasn't even attacking her in the first place.

Strange two-legged creature.

Content to watch from afar, Noel felt safest when she was alone, protected by multiple fences from whatever odd things this human decided to do next.

Certainly, the human was weird.

But it would be okay if she came back with more bananas.

January 22, 2018
Black Forest, Colorado
Two Years, Five Months Captive
Eight Months Rescued
Nineteen Days Home

January 22nd was my first day shift in over a year. I hadn't slept overnight because my body was wondering why we weren't at work pounding stale coffee. I had dragged myself out of bed before sunrise and spent eight hours at the hospital, shadowing orthopedic cases in the operating room. I was a zombie by the time I left at 3:15 P.M., but I wanted to use the remaining ninety minutes of daylight to check in on the girls at the barn.

Noel had grown accustomed to having her own banana as an appetizer in the early morning hours before her hay arrived, and there was no way for me to explain to her that "after work" now meant the evening time.

Exhausted, I sat with Noel without any expectations and simply observed her behaviors and the way she interacted with the world.

She was timid, but not an outcast, defiantly unwilling to cower in the corner and let me idly spy on her. Noel had grown more interested in socializing with me. Food was her biggest motivating factor. She would take snacks from my hand as long as I extended my arm as far as I could, and didn't make eye contact with her during the process.

Time spent in close proximity led to Noel accepting human touch on her shoulder- but only her shoulder. If my hand moved closer to her head, legs, or midsection, she scrambled away. It was her shoulder or nothing.

Days of nothing but quick contact with her shoulder eventually became short windows of time when she would tolerate contact with her neck. Soon, I could touch her hip. Then, the coveted forehead rub, although her ears would flop to the back of her head every time my hand came towards her eyes.

Forehead rubs led to cheek rubs, which led my hand to touching her halter. Over the course of a few weeks, tolerating my hands on her halter eventually evolved into manipulating the buckles on her halter, which made me wonder if January 22nd was the day to remove her Nylon halter.

She'd had a halter affixed to her face for quite some time. The thought of removing it was scary to some extent- what if I couldn't get it back on? What if she escaped again? What if I scared her in the process of taking the halter off and our progress digressed?

Leaving a Nylon halter on an equine comes with its own list of risks, too, though. Halters can get caught on solid objects such as fence posts, causing the animal to panic when it realizes it's been trapped, and serious injury, even death, can be the result.

I had reached a crossroads, and realized that I'd quickly adopted an attitude of "meh" when it came to trying new things with Noel. The reality check that she was so significantly different than any horse I'd ever met had knocked me all the way back to square one. The combination of realizing that I had a lot to learn before I could do right by the little burro and the way that she consistently acted in ways I hadn't predicted had led me to coping by shrugging and taking a deep breath when things didn't go according to plan. "Meh."

The timing felt right. She was relaxed, and I had a pocketful of cookies, the two biggest factors that had consistently impacted the outcome of our time spent together. The only two factors that had shown any consistency whatsoever.

Fiddling with her halter, she was unresponsive- the reaction I'd been hoping she'd have. I unbuckled the strap near her throat, keeping a poker face in an attempt to send the message that I didn't care about the outcome. Then, completely separating the throat latch from the crown piece, I let gravity help me slide the nosepiece over her soft muzzle.

There it was.

Her face.

Free.

She acted like nothing had changed. And, nothing had. She couldn't see the halter from the perspective of her own eyeballs, and it probably didn't feel much different on her face due to the handfuls of thick winter hair that padded her head. The change had to be mostly psychological. An unrestrained face.

It took me a minute of sitting on the familiar-but-still-quite-uncomfortable overturned bucket to realize that it was only a psychological change for me, seeing her face with the hair still depressed across her cheeks in the shape of a ghost halter. I was the only one who perceived her as being more free without a physical contraption buckled securely around her face.

I hadn't thought the burro was "free" on Day One when she was enclosed securely in Belle's pen. But, despite her pretending to be confined, she had known the whole time that she could escape if the situation warranted such a reaction. She looked confined, standing within walls six feet tall on each side with multiple strong strands of cable stretching post to post. What I hadn't realized is that she had already sized up each potential gap and had formulated a plan that she knew she could implement without hesitation.

How limited my perceptions are when my only source of information is what I physically see before me.

She was no more confined wearing a halter than she was without it.

She was always free. Freedom is a mindset, not a state of physically being unconfined. And, with roots permanently entwined with those of the sagebrush in southern California, she would always feel free.

February 3, 2018
Black Forest, Colorado
Two Years, Six Months Captive
Nine Months Rescued
One Month Home

I'd promised her a month without judgment, an entire month without allowing myself to assess our progress or even considering the fleeting thought of whether I had bitten off more than I could chew.

The last day of our first month had ended.

The sun rose, and I didn't think about it.

By the time the sun set, I still hadn't taken a step back to fully analyze the situation.

Because there was no situation. Nothing to think about. It had been decided in a thousand little moments throughout the month. She was mine, I took full responsibility for her success, and I refused to let her fail.

So we proceeded as if nothing had changed.

Because nothing had.

February 5, 2018
Colorado Springs, Colorado
Two Years, Six Months Captive
Nine Months Rescued
One Month, Two Days Home

Neonatal emergency resuscitation class, the hardest way to start a Monday morning. Reaching the bottom of my coffee cup before the first module was over didn't bode well for my ability to concentrate for the remainder of the presentation.

Less review, more of the new, I chanted in my head. My sleepy brain couldn't handle another refresher on providing quality CPR. I needed something engaging before my mind started to drift.

People who don't work in health care seem to think that nurses' responses to emergencies mirrors what they see on television. Ranging from making an accurate diagnosis within seconds of laying eyes upon a sick patient to experimenting with radical interventions to save a life, TV medicine might look like an abstract dance requiring creative ideas and on-the-spot innovation on the parts of the nurses and physicians, or, at its most mundane, at least a secret chain of decision-making committed entirely to memory and known only to those trained in the industry.

The truth is quite the opposite. Medical emergencies have been researched and fine-tuned extensively, and evidence-based practice not only dictates every action that nurses and physicians should take, but also changes regularly when new evidence surfaces that could better improve patient outcomes. As such, every time a patient takes a turn for the worse, there is generally a black-and-white algorithm that should be followed to provide rapid intervention to the declining individual. With practice, the exact steps to take in case of an emergency are committed to memory, but it's never wrong to reference flowsheets and reminders of what to do.

Sitting in class to refresh my memory of actions to take in the event an infant needed resuscitation, then, was more akin to sitting in math class than anything else. It requires a certain state of mind to focus on thinking critically about specific ranges of vital signs and medication dosages. Working full-time in health care mandated that I restrict any outside-the-box thinking to the times when I had to creatively convince a screaming four-year-old to take his medicine. There was no room for free thinking around the bedside of a declining patient.

I spent the day at work pounding my mind into submission. *Conform, conform, conform. Leave your own thoughts at the door.* Thankful my Monday shift was just eight hours long instead of twelve, I escaped as quickly as I could at 3:15 P.M., but no earlier or I'd be written up and fired.

Such a positive, supportive work environment.

Finally, freedom of thought. I could talk about whatever struck my fancy, react however I felt appropriate, and fabricate my own unique ideas.

Noel had made progress, significantly so. I could remove and replace her halter with relative ease, and I could touch her legs almost all the way to her knees. She was still fearful and timid, reacting explosively in new or unexpected situations, but I could clip a rope on her halter and walk with her for a few steps before she would throw the weight of her body against the halter in a usually-successful attempt to flee.

But, all of our work was done in the safety of Belle's pen. She got free so often that it still made me nervous to think about taking her into an open space. I didn't want to lose her again.

The arena was the holy grail to my mind's eye when I imagined our success. Great things are accomplished in the arena. In the open space of the large outdoor arena, Noel and I could work on walking long distances softly on a lead rope, trotting, lunging, hopping over jumps, desensitizing to loud, scary objects such as flapping tarps, and more. The possibilities were endless... if I could just get her to the arena.

With the objective goal of arriving to the arena crowding other thoughts from my mind, I worked out a plan to make it happen. I ruled out simply leading her on a rope- we had tried it. Walking with me in new areas was frightening for her, and she always thought she knew best how to keep herself alive, so she'd rip the rope from my hands at the first inkling that I was leading her to someplace she didn't want to be going.

I wondered if she would follow Belle. They were bonding, slowly, more of accepting one another as roommates than becoming inseparable friends. Still, I felt that the bond wasn't strong enough to keep Noel glued to Belle's hip if she got nervous along the way. Plus, I didn't have an extra set of hands to help lead Belle. Joe was tied up at work until after dark every day, and fellow boarders at the barn were busy with their own projects. I would have to find another way.

An off-the-wall idea occurred to me, and felt innovative at the time. I realized, thinking backwards through the problem, that I would need to create a reward system to motivate Noel to walk to the arena. Only a month into my tenure as a donkey owner, I had already realized that "because I said so" is a logic that appeals only to submissive horses. Noel needed a reason to leave the safety of her dojo and accompany me into the great unknown. Food had been her biggest motivator- but how could I communicate to her that there was a food reward waiting at the end of our short walk through the open area?

She was incredibly smart, and I could recognize traits that other donkey owners had described as a photographic memory. She already associated the rubber feed pan with snacks. If I picked it up, she would expect me to place it back on the ground with a cookie inside.

I wondered if I could elicit the same response if I picked the feed pan up and placed it down a foot further away than usual. Or three feet. Or three yards.

If I could instill the idea that the feed pan always contained a delicious reward, I could create a quasi-target system in which I could create a trail of feed pans leading to the arena. If she recognized that all she had to do was walk to each feed pan to find a reward, maybe I could train her to follow the trail of feed pans.

Ridiculous, Future Me would end up captioning in the memory.

But I had few other choices at the time. So I moved forward with the target-training idea, even thinking through the obstacle of making the targets more visible against the sandy terrain than a plain black feed pan. I found a solution at Dollar Tree- bright, multi-colored ceramic plates. They would definitely stand out so that Noel could easily see the next target.

I started the project in her pen, adding banana slices to each plate. She walked around and collected all of the snacks from the plates, time and time again, until I felt that she was ready to try the same task outside her pen.

I set up the trail of plates on February 5th after work, prepping each one with a small pile of banana slices. Then I haltered Noel, a task that I could accomplish in just a few minutes by this time, and led her for the first time through the gate and into the open aisleway. She could run in any direction and find an entrance to the rest of the world. I gripped the rope tight just thinking about the less-than-desirable outcomes that could occur.

Noel was nervous, too. There's no way to know now if her heightened sense of awareness was all her own, or if my tense muscles and anxious subconscious contributed to her state of mind.

"Okay, let's go," I prompted, my sights set on the first target, about six feet ahead of us.

Noel's attention was focused anywhere but on the trail of plates. Alert, wary, she first surveyed the pen nearest us, where a tall palomino Walking Horse named Traveler often draped a friendly head over the fence.

He wasn't friendly in Noel's eyes.

He was a threat to her safety.

She sidled up to the opposite fence as far away from Traveler as she could get, continuing to scope out her environment outside the safety of her comfortable pen.

I gave her half a minute to look around before asking her to move forward again. She resisted, twitching her tail and moving backwards instead of forward, so I kept applying a small amount of pressure on the halter with the lead rope until she finally changed direction.

We made it to the first plate and she gobbled the banana slices as quickly as possible. She didn't take the time to taste them the way she did when she was at liberty in her pen.

In the end, I allowed the tense burro to return to her home before we even made it to the second plate in the trail of six. Watching her retire to the furthest, most isolated corner of her pen, I wondered how I was ever going to get Noel to the arena for training.

I understand now how fatally flawed my strategy to create a trail of targets was from the beginning. No function of learning to follow the trail was going to better Noel. She was not going to learn anything from snacking on a succession of bananas other than the fact that bananas are tasty- a fact she'd established on Day One.

In a small-picture sense, the skills that we needed to add to our repertoire before we could successfully navigate a journey to the arena included all of the most basic principles. Noel needed to become more comfortable yielding the pressure I applied with the halter when asking her to move. She needed to trust me as a handler more, to have faith that I was taking us somewhere safe. She needed to become desensitized to the sights and sounds we would encounter along the way, including leashed dogs jogging past us, tarps flapping, new horses eyeing her warily, and the sudden appearance of vehicles if other boarders happened to arrive at the time we were embarking upon our trip.

The big picture, of course, was that the arena was by no means the end-all, be-all of our training. I had an idea at the time that arriving at the arena would change the dynamic of our working partnership, that we would be approaching "domestic donkey" status if we started working together in the arena rather than the "wild burro" status we maintained as long as we were confined to the much smaller abode where she slept.

Both pictures were blurry to me at the time. Retrospect confirms that I needed a complete reset, a step away from life as I knew it, to fully develop the picture in my mind. But I'm not sure how I could have forced my mind to open up and consider an alternative at the time.

In February of 2018, my best waking hours were stifled in an environment where innovation was frowned upon. Breaking written policy was forbidden and there were no circumstances where I was allowed to exercise my own opinion. I reported to a manager so incompetent she wasn't even aware of her own shortcomings, and came into work each day with her head held high because she was under the illusion that she was well-liked by her subordinates.

Biting my tongue when I wanted to speak out against injustice or make sensible suggestions was soul-crushing, and my creativity was the first victim to the circumstance. I was doing the best I could do at the time, but it's far from the way I would approach the situation given the chance for a do-over. My next wild burro(s) will reap the benefits of their new owner having made all her mistakes from trying to figure out how to train Noel.

Philosophically, if I could go back in time, my do-over would allow much more grace.

I would tell myself that my goals were too lofty and that I was trying to do too much, too fast. I would prioritize setting Noel up in a situation that allows her to figure out the solution on her own, rather than setting up a situation and then trying to tell her how to perform.

Specifically, in a do-over, I would break down the task "walk Noel to the arena" into a hundred smaller tasks that we could work through together. All of them could be done in her pen, because I realized later that the arena held no magic powers. For a young burro learning how to live in domestication, the world was her arena. We could have performed each of the first hundred steps inside the safety of her pen to help her build confidence both in me and in herself.

To start, another month or two, or more, of learning how to submit to pressure would have benefited our journey. I should have spent more time simply applying a halter, pulling on it very slightly with a rope, and waiting for her to figure out that moving her body forward even a millimeter would result in me releasing the pressure I was applying to her face. No, it shouldn't have even required a full step forward to earn the reward of pressure release, although it would take me another few months to learn that component.

I felt like it was time to move forward. In reality, it would have been the perfect time to slow down and build a relationship before moving on to the next step. I didn't realize how much a bonded, trusting partnership would change the way Noel perceived the world when I removed her from the place where she felt safe.

Next time around, I'll take more time to take my time.

February 7, 2018
Black Forest, Colorado
Two Years, Six Months Captive
Nine Months Rescued
One Month, Four Days Home

It was cute, I thought, watching Noel's reaction to meeting the new water trough for the first time.

She'd been drinking out of buckets in a more isolated corner of her pen, and the large rubber water trough sitting halfway between Belle's paddock and her neighbor's pen was a brand new sight.

With Belle shuffled to another paddock for a little while, Noel had free range of the entire pen to explore. My long hours spent wrestling the fencing had resulted in a relatively escape-proof pen, so I was happy to let Noel wander freely and acquaint herself with her new environment.

She had never had the entire area to explore. I stood back, watching her work through her fears, standing on her tiptoes, craning her neck forward, arching it in a manner that would extend her nostrils as far forward as they could go without her having to move her feet any closer.

She snorted quietly, breathing deeply, shuffling left, then shuffling right. It was comical at first. It didn't occur to me until I re-watched the video of the ordeal how much fear she must have been experiencing.

A huge, scary new object, and no herd to rely upon to help her decide if it was safe or dangerous. A terrifying, unidentified blob locked into the paddock with her, and no escape.

A drawn-out, in-depth assessment of the situation concluded with the fact that the water trough must be safe. Ten minutes after starting her approach, Noel was able to dip her chin into the water and take a long, refreshing drink.

Another crisis averted on the long road to making a home at a horse stable.

Valentine's Day 2018
Black Forest, Colorado
Two Years, Six Months Captive
Nine Months Rescued
One Month, Eleven Days Home

A winter wonderland.

The most beautiful kind of Valentine's Day- fresh snow, gray skies, and chilly temperatures.

I knew a large Valentine's pizza, a fireplace, and two snuggly pups would warm me up as soon as I got home, but first, a Valentine's trip to the barn was, of course, necessary.

Pans full of cookies and one-on-one attention with Belle and Noel was our version of celebration. But I could hardly resist the gorgeous allure of the frosted forest beckoning from just over the hill.

"Let's go enjoy the view," I prompted Belle, slipping her halter over her head and guiding her through the gate.

Noel watched silently, thoughtfully, from the back of her section of the pen.

"Someday, girl, we'll all be able to go on walks together."

Unblinking intrigue met me in return.

Belle and I walked up the hill with small, slow-falling flakes dancing past our flushed faces on their downward spirals. Never one to turn down a free meal, Belle nudged the fresh blanket of snow aside to find browned strands of grass to nibble.

We only lasted a few minutes before the cold drove us back inside. Walking down the hill, I could see Noel with her brown eyes still trained on us. She wasn't panicking at Belle's absence, nor did Belle exhibit any qualms about leaving her adopted Friend behind.

I was glad to see Noel watching us, but wondered if their mutual lack of nerves meant they weren't bonding.

"You're kind of stuck with each other," I lectured the girls once they were standing side by side with the fence between them. "I kind of need this to work out between you two."

I sounded like a marriage counselor. A socialist marriage counselor who's really bad at her job.

Belle nickered, slightly, just enough to make her upper lip shiver as she uttered a throaty whisper.

"Yes, you can have another cookie."

February 19, 2018
Black Forest, Colorado
Two Years, Six Months Captive
Nine Months Rescued
One Month, Sixteen Days Home

"I got you a gift."
"Oh, yay!" I clapped. "What is it?"
"You'll see."

Joe returned to his truck to fetch my gift while I crowded around the front window with Max and Audrey.

"Here it is..."

"Oh, it's perfect! Thank you!"

Audrey's nose twitched, sniffing the odd new object, then she walked away, unamused.

I reached out to grab the bright orange traffic cone that Joe was extending towards me. I'd been reading more books and online forums about donkeys, and found multiple different people raving about how much their donkeys enjoyed playing with traffic cones as toys. Apparently, lots of donkeys love knocking them over and dragging them around.

I had been looking forward to presenting Noel with a new traffic cone that I was sure would be an instant hit, solidifying my status as a fun and trustworthy human in Noel's life.

I drove tossed it in my car to drive north right away. The thirty-five-minute drive to the barn felt like a long and arduous journey, but at long last, I found myself rolling under the Pine Run Ranch archway.

Belle's pen looked different now, set up to accommodate both Belle and Noel as safely as possible. The round pen panels that had divided Belle's paddock in half had been broken down into pairs and then folded into V-shaped partitions that separated a generous parcel of dirt where Belle could enjoy her hay in solidarity from another corner where Noel could stay out of the way during meal times. There had been no further problems since Day One, but we erred on the side of caution during high-energy events like anticipating the feed truck.

"Girls!" I blurted excitedly. I let myself into the pen through the gate with the traffic cone under my arm. "We got a new cone!"

I proudly placed the orange traffic cone in the center of the pen. Belle barely blinked an eye, turning instead towards my pockets to search for tasty morsels. Noel stood back, unamused.

"Donkeys are supposed to love playing with these things," I informed Noel.

A blank stare met me in return.

I rocked the cone back and forth to garner more attention. "See," I continued my sales pitch.

Noel blinked.

I've never worked in sales. If I had, I may have starved.

"You don't like it?" I asked Noel, hands on my hips.

Snort.

"Can you at least pose with it so I send a picture to your father?"

Blink.

"Wait, I know." I unpeeled a banana I'd been reserving for Noel, finally capturing her interest. Rather than offer up the treat, however, I tucked it underneath the cone and took a step back.

Not usually one to fall for tricks, I was surprised I'd won the game this time. Noel stepped up the plate and arched her neck, lining her nostril up with the top of the cone. I was able to snap a quick picture before Noel knocked the cone over to fetch her prize.

"Did she like the cone?" Joe asked upon my return to the house.

"Well... I got this picture."

"She looks interested in it!"

"I had to bribe her by hiding a banana in it," I confessed.

Joe shook his head with a smile. "She has you trained."

"No..." I started to protest.

But I didn't have any kind of argument to defend myself against his accusation. Perhaps I hadn't won the game at all. Noel didn't fall for any kind of trick. She got a free banana for doing nothing more than walking up to a new object that she didn't even find to be scary.

"Maybe the secret to training a donkey is to do the opposite of whatever my first instinct is," I pondered aloud.

Surely, it wouldn't hurt, since my instincts were doing a poor job of setting me up for success.

Embrace the antithesis.

I needed a new theme song for this chapter of donkmanship.

March 9, 2018
Black Forest, Colorado
Two Years, Seven Months Captive
Ten Months Rescued
Two Months, Six Days Home

Steering down the highways crisscrossing from I-25 to the barn at sixty miles an hour, I occasionally drove past large sections of burned forest ravaged by fire in 2013. The once-towering pines clung crookedly to dead roots, charred black, the undergrowth missing, serving as a reminder of the extremes that Colorado weather can inflict even upon those who love it.

Over five hundred homes burned in Black Forest in 2013. At the beginning of 2018, weather conditions started to check all the blocks required by Mother Nature to spark another major disaster. Snowpack in the mountains was well below average, and precipitation refused to fall on thirsty fields.

I had a happy burro and an ambivalent mare on my hands. Having originated in a dry climate, Noel was far from upset to spend her days in a dry, sandy paddock. In fact, too much moisture can cause donkeys to sprout painful abscesses in their hooves.

My own anxiety was beginning to climb, however. I proficiently channeled my nerves into action when faced with conditions that I feel I have some ability to influence, but the climate and weather forecast was far from my control. So, I stressed about it instead, keeping an obsessive eye on the seven-day predictions and getting upset when careless humans sparked small fires that quickly grew into catastrophic conditions.

The ranch where I boarded held a meeting to discuss the evacuation plan.

The antidote to anxiety is a well-laid plan. It was somewhat of a relief to know that my animals were in the hands of long-time Colorado residents who had experienced many fire seasons and knew exactly how to respond. With family in law enforcement, they were well-connected to breaking news in the area. Multiple rigs were at their disposal if the need arose to evacuate more than thirty equine. Places to shelter the evacuated animals were lined up in every direction so that decisions could be made based on where a potential wildfire would be travelling.

A call-to-action rang in my ears when I heard that Belle and Noel would be at the bottom of the list for evacuations.

Someone has to be the last to leave the property, after all, so some animals were inevitably going to bring up the bottom of the list. It made sense that I didn't have my own trailer, so I'd be relying on two empty slots in someone else's vehicle. Making a mental note to throw all of my available resources at a savings account for my own rig, the next piece of logic hit me even harder.

"We'll prioritize loading up the animals that we know will get on the trailers quickly. Then, when we come back for Belle and Noel, we can take all the time we have left to coax Noel onto the trailer."

An immediate wave of guilt hit me. Belle, the easygoing, easy-to-manage mare who would load within seconds onto any trailer with an open door, was handicapped by the Forever Friend I'd gifted her.

I'd chosen a wild burro, rather selfishly, instead of a trained miniature horse. A tame mini who loaded quickly may have gotten Belle and an already-domestic Forever Friend closer to the top of the list of evacuees. But my choices had the potential to affect Belle's outcome during a catastrophic disaster.

I took responsibility for creating the handicap, but knew also that I had the power to change it.

My motivation to hurry Noel's progress along renewed, we kept working, and I kept asking for more.

At least, by March, I'd learned that training was truly a question I had to ask, not a task I could mandate. Observation and an overwhelming desire to improve had helped shape my training sessions. I continued to use positive reinforcement and recognize what I thought were small tries on Noel's behalf.

I'd come to realize that the behaviors I thought of as the smallest try were not broken down into small enough segments. Again, I was applying too many ingrained horse behavior techniques to the training of an animal that was not a horse.

It's not easy to undo nearly two decades of understanding. I wondered if it would have been easier to have less horse experience so that I wouldn't default to reacting in certain ways. I imagined it must be similar to owning house cats for a number of years and then adopting a puma.

The only way to move forward, though, is to move forward.

So forward we went.

March 19, 2018
Black Forest, Colorado
Two Years, Seven Months Captive
Ten Months Rescued
Two Months, Sixteen Days Home

The second week of March marked Spring Break for lots of schools. It was more or less irrelevant to me, given that I wasn't in a traditional school system for my graduate studies and that I didn't have human children, but my mom worked for a school in Indiana and enjoyed the same breaks as the students. For Spring Break 2018, she planned another trip West.

My parents had been in town enough times before to generate a virtual list of favorite places to revisit in town. Indulging in large breakfasts at King's Chef Diner was always a priority, as were blackberry mocha lattes to accompany road trips into the mountains.

This trip, however, was the first time that the newest member of our family, my parents' grand-burro, was home.

I prioritized a family trip to the barn as soon as my parents were rested enough from their travels.

I had an ulterior motive.

"Would one of you mind leading Belle to the arena so Noel and I can follow?"

I wasn't sure how it would go- I wasn't sure what kind of disaster could ensue from an attempt to cross a wide open stretch of land. But I was itching to try. I still had delusions of grandeur related to the leaps and bounds of success The Arena was going to help us unleash.

I had a willing party, and we set out on an adventure.

As full-fledged of a unicorn as she'd ever been, Belle trod placidly alongside whomever was holding her rope.

More bonded to the big bay mare by mid-March, Noel was not about to be separated from Belle. She pranced nervously beside me, her focus trained on her big sister. It likely didn't foster any feeling of calmness that my hands trembled slightly with my own nerves on the way up the hill.

Please don't get loose.

Please don't run away.

The sigh of relief I breathed when we reached the gate to the arena made me realize that I'd been holding my breath for some time.

And the potential for disaster wasn't over yet.

A virtual shrug of my shoulders christened Noel's debut into the arena as I unclipped the rope from her halter.

She had more room to run than she'd had since the night of the Great Escape.

And run she did.

First, an upright trot, head held high, turning circles to survey her new stomping ground. Then her trot extended, her knees snapping towards her narrow chest, her tiny hooves making a more pronounced crunch as they punched the sand.

She stopped, looking, sniffing, surveying.

Then, like the snap of a rubber band, she was off to the races, galloping as if she had just burst forth from the starting gate at the Preakness.

Her energy was contagious, and Belle left her post at the edge of the arena where the grass grew to join her Friend in her antics.

Ever since she came home to me as a yearling, Belle had a tendency to poke her nose as high as she could manage into the sky when she ran.

"She'll grow out of it," trainers told me at first.

A year later, their comments transitioned. "That's odd, I've never seen another horse run like that. Hopefully it's just a phase."

Later still, the conversation turned to, "what's wrong with your mare? Why does she run like that?"

"Oh, that's just Belle."

Fifteen years later, she kicked up her heels, racing down the fence line with her tail flying like a flag, her nose still turned straight upwards towards the sun.

Noel flew alongside her, lacking the natural-born magnificence of a flowing mane and tail that most horses showcase without even trying, but radiant instead in her own unique way. Her body type was different, too. Smooth layers of muscle comprised her narrow frame, appearing less visually strong than a horse that had bulging clusters of rounded muscles, but exhibiting her power nonetheless in her speed as her haunches drew far underneath her mass.

One lap they made, then two, stride after stride of pure joy and freedom.

Then Noel did what all little sisters do.

She wanted to be like Belle.

On lap number three, Noel galloped alongside Belle in harmony.

And then tipped her nose straight up towards the sun.

March 31, 2018
Black Forest, Colorado
Two Years, Seven Months Captive
Ten Months Rescued
One Month, Twenty-Eight Days Home

"We did it once," I reminded the girls.

Belled nosed my pockets for cookies, oblivious to the butterflies fluttering nearby in my gut.

I clenched her rope in my left hand, and Noel's in my right. Never mind that Belle wasn't used to walking on my left side- I was less nervous about her thousand pounds finding their way on the wrong side of me than I was about Noel's five hundred pounds staying on my right.

Laser-focused on the arena, we made it.

The Arena, the magical land where all of our dreams were going to come true.

If I had the ability to re-watch the incredible feat of my first time leading fifteen hundred pounds of equine across the barnyard singlehandedly, I'm sure it would be even more awe-inspiring after the fact.

Because Noel probably mustered a thousand times more courage than I gave her credit for.

She bravely walked past her palomino neighbors, all three of them, the boys who made her wary.

She resisted the urge to flee when we reached the open, fenceless portion of our walk.

She didn't pull away to eat the grass growing beside us.

She never thought of kicking or biting the human tugging on her head and telling her to walk more slowly.

She kept her wits, and trusted the strange person who kept asking her to do ridiculous tasks.

She had every opportunity to bolt.

To stop listening to my cues.

To succumb to her fears.

But she stayed.

She obeyed.

And we made it.

The Arena.

Her lesson should have been done long before we reached the white gate.

But she humored me.

Undeserving, clueless, closed-minded me.

Retrospect made me realize that I got a good one.

April 4, 2018
Black Forest, Colorado
Two Years, Eight Months Captive
Eleven Months Rescued
Three Months, One Day Home

Few and far between are the mares that remain consistent under saddle even when they haven't been worked regularly in months. But Belle wasn't so much a mare as she was a unicorn.

Riding used to be the epitome of horse ownership for me. I spent almost every day in the saddle, logging hours every week. Belle and I rode in arenas, on trails, on roads, and in harvested fields. There weren't many places Belle wouldn't agree to go.

Work responsibilities, school responsibilities, and other various aspects of Army spouse life, however, left me seeking a place to relax and unwind, which usually didn't include taking the time or energy to groom and saddle Belle.

Other days, however, I still craved the freedom of sitting astride my well-worn saddle. It was new-to-me, seventy-five dollars at an antique shop in Victor, Colorado. I bought it expecting to turn a profit reselling it, but it ended up fitting both me and Belle perfectly, and I kept it.

I had grand thoughts of one day ponying Noel alongside Belle, riding the trails independently, with Belle's days of buddy sourness a distant memory.

Someday, of course, when I had more time.

I saddled Belle and escorted both girls to the arena in the same nerve-wracking rhythm we'd come to know over the course of a few solo trips. I never knew if something would set Noel off, or if she would end up getting loose.

But she never went far anymore.

She didn't want to be out of sight from her sister.

After a relatively-uneventful arrival to the arena, I turned Noel loose. She loved bathing in the sand, stretching her legs, and grazing along the grass growing at the edges of the arena.

Easygoing Belle stood for me to swing aboard. I adjusted the reins, wondering if Noel's antics would excite Belle. A few minutes into our slow walk along the rail, though, Belle assured me that she was unconcerned with Noel's shenanigans.

Rounding the corner to start our second lap, I realized that Noel wasn't playing in the same manner that she usually did. Instead, she was fixated on what was happening, ears alert, eyes astonished.

Unable to believe that Belle was okay with all this.

It didn't look okay.

She may have encountered horseback riders before, either in the Chemehuevi area of California or in a holding facility. If she had seen someone atop a horse, their goal was likely to apply pressure to her to make her move.

She was quick to move away from that kind of pressure.

But Belle and I weren't pressure.

The mental struggle of whether to flee or approach us was likely making her brain do flips, so she did neither, staying frozen.

A few more laps and I hopped off Belle. It was enough exposure for one day.

"It's going to be awhile before you'll pony alongside us, isn't it."

Inquisitive brown eyes blinked.

"That's okay. Take your time."

April 5, 2018
Black Forest, Colorado
Two Years, Eight Months Captive
Eleven Months Rescued
Three Months, Two Days Home

I even hated the thought of calling the dentist to make an appointment for myself, and I am a healthy human perfectly capable of sitting still in a dentist's office. I just don't enjoy it. I get annoyed every time the hygienist asks me a question while my mouth is pried open with dental instruments. I spend ninety percent of the appointment holding my breath until the cleaning is complete.

And I grew up going to the dentist. I know that I have a 100 percent track record of surviving dental appointments. I'd endured easily in excess of forty dental cleanings by April of 2018.

So, then, scheduling an appointment for a burro who had far less desire to endure a painless procedure than I had to endure a dental cleaning gnawed a pit in my stomach.

But it was time to schedule a routine hoof trimming for Noel.

I prefaced my request to new, potential farriers with a detailed explanation of Noel's status as a wild burro and our current level of training: questionable and inconsistent at best.

The universe was on my side.

I reached a nationally renowned expert in the field of donkey trimming on my first try.

Thanks, Google!

May 15th would officially be our first farrier appointment.

Feelings of dread and instant regret met me. *It's not going to work. She's not going to be ready.*

Maybe I should figure out how to do it myself before then.

I better get started trying right now.

One thirty-five-minute drive later, I was face-to-face with my opposition.

Small, hard, round donkey hooves. The things of kicking, striking, and stomping, I'd thought once upon a time.

It seemed that Noel didn't want me down there any more than I wanted to be there. I was making good progress with being able to contact other parts of her body, but I could not get below her knees. All I could picture was my face caved in on one side, the deadly result of a single powerful kick landed on my cheek.

I was even less inclined to try to get below her hocks on her rear legs.

I received a suggestion from the barn owner and I put it into practice. She suggested that I could loop a long rope around Noel's pastern and then gently twist the rope to take the slack out, thereby preventing it from slipping off her foot. I could then stand near her head, safely, where Noel was more comfortable and gently apply pressure with the rope until I lifted her foot off the ground.

I found a piece of soft cotton rope, and was able to drape the rope around Noel's pasterns without her getting too upset. It seems that she was less upset by me looping the rope around her legs than if I was trying to touch her legs with my hands. That preference should have told me that it wasn't contact with her legs that she was upset about, but rather just the closeness of me and my hand to her feet.

Regardless, I thought at the time that I was making good progress by working towards picking her feet up. I slowly pushed her out of her comfort zone and got closer to holding her foot in my hands. At about the same point every time, however, she continued to get tense and move away as quickly as possible when I started bending towards her foot.

Donkey feet do not grow particularly fast, I had learned. I was spoiled by good feet. I had gotten away with only a few farrier visits per year for Belle even with her softer, faster-growing domestic horse hooves. But I was so concerned about the ability to trim Noel's feet that it seems they were growing right before my eyes.

I wondered why it hadn't occurred to me to line up professionals like donkey farriers and veterinarians before I brought a wild burro home. I had been so confident that I was going to make more mature decisions at this point in my life before I adopted a new animal. But, I was realizing that 2017 Me had been overcome by the fairy tale, once again.

Now, playing catch up, I had valid concerns.

I needed to be able to pick up all of Noel's feet in about five weeks.

I couldn't even pick up one.

April 12, 2018
Black Forest, Colorado
Two Years, Eight Months Captive
Eleven Months Rescued
Three Months, Nine Days Home

I expressed my concerns about our impending First Trim to our veterinarian on the day that she came out for annual vaccinations.

Per her recommendations, I purchased a horse-sized dose of dormosedan gel. I was thankful to have an option in my back pocket, but I wasn't even sure I would be able to administer the medication. I read about its administration online. Even working as a nurse and passing dozens of medications every day that I was on duty, I felt wary of my ability to apply the sedative in Noel's mouth.

It wasn't that long ago, on a typical night shift, that we had to chemically restrain a demented psych patient.

It is always hard to predict how a mental health patient is going to react to, who they are going to trust, or what behaviors they will exhibit from minute to minute. The patient was not even in my primary care. But as "just another" nurse on the unit who entered the room when the patient became combative, my face became the one that he gravitated towards as someone trustworthy. It just happens like that sometimes, unpredictably. Then, after a sequence of events, with two security officers physically restraining the patience for his own safety, I was the one who administered a mild sedative through his intravenous catheter.

Many things can go wrong in this kind of scenario. I could have lost all trust with the patients and he could have become aggressive with me. The patients could have yanked free of the men holding him down and ripped his IV out, eliminating the best access point for the medication to be given. A paradoxical reaction could have occurred in response to the medication, worsening the situation for all of us. Or, any number of potential side effects could have occurred, creating a medical emergency.

Yet, I had been more confident administering that dose of medication than I was with the thought of getting dormosedan gel under Noel's tongue in a way that it could be effective to mildly sedate her.

But I didn't have much time to dwell on the potential impending problem of dormosedan administration after Noel received her shots. The shots themselves hadn't gone well. After Belle flawlessly stood still, accepting three separate shots in her neck without issue, Noel had been less agreeable. When the first needle pierced her thick hide, her explosive objection had caused the needle to bend inside her neck, likely inflicting considerable pain, and causing visible trauma to the site that resulted in a large, swollen knot.

With two shots still to be administered, the veterinarian had to restrain Noel for her own safety by attaching a rope to Noel's halter and fastened it snugly to the fence post.

If she'd been more tame it may have not been necessary to restrain her to that extent.

It wasn't the best option. But it was the best option we had.

There were stocks at the barn, but we had never practiced with them, or even walked to that portion of the barn. It would have been kind of a toss-up as to what was the least stressful way to get the vaccinations into her body.

She wanted out so badly that she was chewing on the cable fencing, gnawing her teeth back and forth, a coping mechanism that ended up causing a gash on her nose. A small enough scrape, just a few big drops of blood, but enough to make me feel terrible, nauseatingly so. The hairline scar is still visible in photographs taken of her face today.

Three drama-laced pokes later, and annual vaccines were behind us-.

Thank goodness.

As I walked out front with the veterinarian to pay my tab, Noel was offended, upset, and sore. I anticipated it being a few days before she would forgive me. I walked back to their pen after swiping my credit card- shots cost me more than the amount of my monthly rent in college- to spend some time with her.

Dinner had been served, and Belle was eating happily. I knew from years past that she would be a little bit sore for a day or two, but she didn't usually have any other side effects.

I returned to my comfortable place on that overturned bucket and watched Noel from afar. She didn't want to come near me, and that was okay. I understood. I talked to her, told her why vaccines are necessary, and explained that even though she was hurting a little bit right now, the discomfort paled in comparison to what she would experience if she contracted a preventable disease and we had to treat her for it. Depending on what she contracted, Noel could potentially have to endure daily needle sticks for weeks and weeks, painful skin eruptions, or neurological symptoms that were completely irreversible, among a long list of other possibilities. I didn't agree with everything in Western medicine, but vaccines had established their value, and they were important.

Admittedly, I had been a little bit traumatized by the event as well, and that's my excuse for not realizing sooner that Noel wasn't indulging in her dinner the same way she did on any other night.

With growing alarm, I looked at her, watched her more closely. I tried to convince myself that I was being paranoid. I did, after all, tend to be more conservative in my assessment of gray areas than other people, jumping more quickly to the "worst case scenario" than other people.

She was standing very closely to the cinder block wall of the shelter, eyes listless, ears not standing upright. She wasn't interested in the pile of hay nearby. Most concerning, though, was that the longer I looked, the more symptoms I started to see.

Was I imagining the swelling?

Was it in my head that she was depressed and withdrawn?

I hoped so.

Briefly.

Then, it hit me quite suddenly that none of it was in my head.

She was sick.

And it was getting worse very quickly.

A phone call to the vet left me feeling like she didn't understand the severity of the situation. I didn't know how to convey it any more clearly. Perhaps she thought I just didn't know what I was talking about. I wasn't panicked enough yet to want to start throwing around titles- I kept my status as a people nurse a secret. I surely didn't want to offend her by making her think I felt that a Registered Nurse knows the same amount of information as a veterinarian. But it was becoming more undeniably clear to me that this animal was having a reaction, a serious one, and that she was in a significant amount of distress. She needed intervention.

Now.

I didn't know how to convey the urgency of the situation and any other words other than what I had already tried to do.

So I paced.

I waited.

And Noel's symptoms worsened in the span of just a few minutes.

She had her eyes closed and her breathing appeared more labored. Every few moments she would arch her neck and tuck her chin towards her chest. Then, she appeared to be putting forth a great effort to swallow. I grew even more panicked, and I wasn't sure how to prioritize my next steps. That same terrible tunnel vision started to blur my periphery. I knew she would need to be caught before any intervention could be performed. But, at the same time, I didn't want to distress her further by trying to put a halter on her when she obviously was already very stressed by her own physical status. I wondered if it was best to wait for the vet to arrive with emergency medications before I put Noel's body through more grief and attempted to capture her again.

As Murphy's Law would have it, the battery on my phone dropped from 70% to 4%. I paced faster to fight back the worry that a veterinarian was not going to arrive in time.

I've never been so thankful to hear the crunching of gravel on the other side of the barn.

I left Noel for just a few seconds to meet the veterinarian at her truck and show her the video that I had taken on my phone of the hard swallowing that Noel was exhibiting.

"Oh, she's choking!" exclaimed the veterinarian.

But she wasn't.

I explained that I had not seen Noel eat any food since the time that we had untied her following her shots. And it would have just been too big of a coincidence that her array of symptoms was occurring within an hour of her having received her vaccines.

The vet drew some dexamethasone into a syringe and joined me in the barnyard. Dex, as it's affectionately nicknamed, is a steroid, and its function is to decrease swelling. It's the same medication that some humans gets when they need intravenous steroids in the hospital.

"Well, this shot will be even more fun because it needs to go in her vein," said the vet.

So, we had no choice.

Capture.

I sighed in relief when I got the halter back on her head.

Confinement, squeezed between the fence a round pen panel that I pressed against her with trembling arms.

Confusion.

She'd never felt like this before.

Clanging, as she fought weakly against her makeshift prison.

She was even more full of fear this time, her neck so wracked with tension that it felt as solid as a brick wall. She knew what was about to happen, that the painful prick of the needle was about to pierce her flesh. It was another one of the countless times I wish I'd been able to communicate with Noel with something other than body language to explain more adequately what was about to happen, and the fact that it was in her best interest- no, that, actually, we didn't have a choice at all.

This time, we used the principle of leverage more in our favor as we strung the ropes around poles on either side of Noel's face, pulling on them to draw her face closer to the fence.

But it still wasn't enough.

The five-hundred-pound animal thought she was fighting for her life, and I couldn't convince her otherwise.

I thought again of how thankful I was that that *this* wasn't my everyday practice in medicine. I could barely stomach doing it for this one animal. I couldn't imagine having an entire day, then an entire week, then an entire career, having to fight animals to do things that they didn't want to be done to them.

Sometimes, even on humans who understand the procedure and are willing to undergo it, I don't hit the vein on people arms on the first try. That's just the way it is. I've never been so thankful to have a vet who was able to hit a vessel that she couldn't even see on the first try on an animal that was fighting us tooth and nail.

An intravenous dose of dexamethasone on board, the vet explained that the medication would start working to reverse Noel's symptoms.

Then she packed up-

Handed me another syringe of dex, *just in case*-

And left.

Where are you going, I thought. *You need to monitor her to make sure that this medication is going to be effective and that she's going to be able to breathe!*

But that's not the way it is in animal medicine.

So I paid the second bill for the day and then returned to the barnyard to monitor Noel myself.

I stayed as far away as I could while still having an eye on her.

Please.

I've never been so acutely aware of the amount of stress that my mere presence caused a creature.

In retrospect, the same awareness of my body language and the way that my physical presence impacted Noel's emotions and mental state of being could have benefited us as I was attempting to train her in the few months prior.

In any case, I was fully aware now.

It worked. The medication did what it was supposed to do. Shortly, Noel was able to drop her head and breathe more easily. The swelling that caused her ears to fall to the side and had engorged her pasterns was starting to go away. She felt well enough that she was able to take a few small bites of hay. I breathed a little more deeply myself.

But I knew it wasn't over. I didn't feel right leaving her. I was so concerned that the steroid was going to wear off and her swelling was going to return. This type of reaction was unprecedented in my experience with animals. I had never seen it. I didn't know if it would come back, how it would affect her the rest of the night, or what to expect.

When it got so dark outside that I could no longer see, I got in my car, hesitantly, and drove home. But I still couldn't rest. I went over Noel's paperwork from the Bureau of Land Management and saw that she had been given all of the same vaccines before. No adverse reaction was noted. I wondered if she'd had the same type of reaction in a holding facility, and whether they would have noticed or medicated her. I wondered if this was her first reaction. I wondered if the paperwork was correct. I wondered if she'd ever come so close to suffocating before. I had so many questions.

At 11:00 P.M., I should have been sleeping. But I couldn't. Despite my exhaustion after the incident occurred, I too worried to rest. I had to make sure she was okay.

The barn was so different in the dark, less welcoming than it was during the day. While I didn't feel scared, per se, I felt a little uneased. Creepy. It wasn't a relaxing place to sit in my car and observe.

The door to the hayloft didn't latch, and it creaked eerily, swinging back and forth, clanging when it made contact with the side of the barn. It was pitch black. There were stars in the sky, but they didn't illuminate anything in the rural countryside. The kind of peaceful that would have been relaxing at dusk, but it was more unsettling in the middle of the night than anything else. I could hear movement all around me. It was just the other horses, surely… but there was no way to know. Large predators had been seen in the same area. It could just as easily have been a mountain lion, or even a bear.

Or, the scariest predator of all, a human.

Most of the time, impulse shopping makes it really easy to waste twenty dollars. Other times, I ended up investing twenty dollars on something that proves to be invaluable. My LED spotlight lamp from Amazon fell into the "priceless" category. It never ran out of battery, and it illuminated everything around it. I could even sit it on the ground and have a small circumference of light so I could see everything around me. In the middle of the night that April, I kept the spotlight trained on Noel.

I slept in my car, kind of, dozing in and out, never sleeping very deeply, with a syringe full of dexamethasone in the cup holder at my ready.

Please don't make me have to use this tonight.
Please be okay.
Please just be okay.

April 13, 2018
Black Forest, Colorado
Two Years, Eight Months Captive
Eleven Months Rescued
One Hundred Days Home

One hundred days.

The landmark in a school year that students and teacher alike celebrate.

The time period in which a new President of the United States is judged for his (or her) early accomplishments.

And, the amount of time that extreme mustang makeover participants have to transform a wild horse into a riding animal and compete in a variety of classes before a big audience, often showing off advanced maneuvers.

For the purpose of competing in mustang gentling competition, in the span of just one hundred days, participants take an animal that started in the same place as Noel, train them, and haul them to a new place, where they compete in a loud, scary arena in front of hundreds, if not thousands, of people.

Incredible.

But, one hundred days is not realistic for every handler, nor every animal. In fact, it's probably unrealistic for the majority of equine and trainers alike.

After college, I was hired to train a couple of horses under saddle. I had done it before. I broke Belle to ride all by myself as an ambitious sixteen-year-old. When Belle was two, I started climbing aboard, applying all of the groundwork we'd worked on together and building upon our relationship, resting upon a solid foundation of trust. It wasn't a huge step up, as Belle took naturally to me sitting atop her back, walking and jogging calmly, listening to all my cues.

It had felt like such a quick turnaround at the time. When Belle was of age, it only took a few weeks to be able to place a full-sized saddle on her back, tighten the girth, put a metal bit in her mouth, and desensitize her to the initially-unbalanced feeling of having a human swing aboard.

There was no bucking, no biting, no bolting. Just laid-back Belle, taking all her new tasks in stride.

In reality, though, I had spent far more than a few weeks getting to that point- months, rather, of groundwork and bonding that I hadn't factored. Having started my partnership with Belle when she was a yearling, we had worked together daily. Even before she was mature enough to ride, I worked with her on standing patiently in cross-ties, being groomed, lunging, leading, desensitizing, worming, and trimming. She calmly accepted various procedures from the veterinarian, such as removal of her wolf teeth and an attempt to flush the tear duct in her right eye. (Interestingly, as it turned out, she didn't have a complete tear duct in her right eye, leading to her tears permanently spilling over her lower lid on the right side of her face, a drainage issue she faces to this day).

All things considered, we'd spent well over a year working together and preparing for a safe transition under saddle. It was not a one-hundred-day transformation.

So, a bit misled as I agreed to breaking a couple young horses, I had started my new project optimistically.

I hadn't realized how slowly I worked, until I was faced with an animal that did not have a strong groundwork foundation and had not built a relationship with me, and was faced with trying to map out a plan for eventually riding that animal safely.

I wasn't progressing very fast, and started to feel like I was failing. Some sessions ended without any headway having been made. I would start out with groundwork, for example, lunging at liberty in a round pen, and work through kinks like inattention or changing direction on a whim, and work until we got to a point where the horse was loping calmly, responding to my body cues, and stopping on command. But, by the time that point in the session arrived, an entire day of work was gone.

Horse people seem to love thirty day increments. "Thirty days of training! Thirty days of rides on him!" But thirty days come and go very quickly, and I've never understood the draw of that particular time increment. "Thirty days" is a quantifier and doesn't speak to the quality of training at all.

At the end of thirty days into my debut into horse training, I still hadn't put a saddle on the horses. I didn't think it was safe, and I didn't think the horses' foundation was solid enough to accommodate progressing to that extent.

I can't say whether those horse trainers who offer a quick thirty day turnaround are wrong, because I haven't seen their progress from start to finish. By the same token, I also can't say whether they're right. But what I learned was that I was never going to make money training horses because few people want to spend six months reaching the same point that a faster trainer can reach in thirty days. Horse people paying the feed bill or monthly board on a half-ton animal want to be able to ride it *now*.

So, as much as I love watching extreme mustang makeovers in complete awe, the one-hundred-day turnaround sets the bar at a level that I'm not capable of attaining. I don't think it's unattainable because my results aren't good, but because I prioritize a strong foundation over speedy progress and work far too cautiously to ever make the cut in one hundred days.

Ever-evolving, maybe I'll surprise myself one day.

But, for now, I'm comfortable with one hundred days being the length of my warm up.

One hundred days into my journey with Noel, and I couldn't have dragged her into an arena to compete if I'd wanted to. But, I could halter her quickly and calmly, and she seemed content, figuring out her new world alongside Belle.

One hundred days into our journey and we were developing our partnership. A success story in the making.

Slowly.

April 14, 2018
Black Forest, Colorado
Two Years, Eight Months Captive
Eleven Months Rescued
Three Months, Twenty Days Home

Recovered. Safe. Healthy.

With all of her edema receded and no lasting evidence of the ordeal she had endured, it was time to carry on with life as usual. I gathered supplies to practice oral medication administration in case we needed to apply the dormosedan under her tongue.

I practiced administering medication into her mouth the way that many horse people practice the same technique with a horse.

Most worming medication comes in a tube that has to be administered into a horse's mouth. So, every six weeks, it's something that must be done to keep the horse and good health.

I once cared for a spirited Appaloosa mare named Bonnie who despised receiving worming medication. Just a teenager at the time, I had read about a trick to encourage horses to take the worming tube into their mouths without a struggle.

Bonnie loved bananas, making her the only equid other than Noel I've met who would steal the fruit from my hand. Interestingly, looking back, Bonnie had a short black mane that stood on end very similar to a donkey's mane, and a short tail that did not touch the ground, about the same length as Noel's. She had a rather difficult, hard-headed demeanor. I attributed all of those traits to her Appaloosa roots at the time, but perhaps a piece of her soul actually belonged to the longear community. Kindred spirits, at the very least.

I had filled empty worming tubes with mashed bananas and then administered the bananas into Bonnie's mouth the same way I hoped to eventually do with worming medication

Fifteen years later, I repeated the trick with Noel, and I was shocked when I was able to administer the first tube of mashed bananas into Noel's mouth without too much of a struggle.

A complete relief!

Then, just to make sure, I filled the tube up again and attempted the procedure a second time.

If it was a horse, it would have been commonplace to ensure that I could perform the procedure to or three times without flaw, before the actual day came that I needed to administer medication through the tube. I did not think twice about making a second attempt.

Noel, however, reminded me once again that she is not a horse and that drilling through mundane tasks is one of the best ways to offend a donkey.

When a donkey is has made up its mind, there is little that can be done to convince the animal otherwise.

More than a year later, I still haven't ever gotten a tube of medication into her mouth again.

April 21, 2018
Black Forest, Colorado
Two Years, Eight Months Captive
Eleven Months Rescued
Three Months, Eighteen Days Home

Four shifts in five days leading up to one glorious Saturday, and I needed a change of pace.

"Let's go on an adventure," I whispered.

Belle nickered. Noel stared.

We hadn't embraced wide, open spaces since the night of the Great Escape. Rather, we walked through them as fast we could to get to other side. But it was time. I needed to breathe.

Combatting my uneasiness about leading Noel into an open field far from her house without a fence to stop her if she fled, I chose her Nylon halter and a sixteen-foot lunge line and filled my pockets with her favorite apple-flavored cookies.

Then, we marched, Belle on my left and Noel on my right, up the hill, past the gate to the arena, and onward to the big, grassy field where I used to ride Belle.

Fresh snow on the ground illuminated the longer blades of grass and produced a soothing quiet crunch when all eight hooves excitedly stepped foot into the open.

Belle dove immediately for grass, inhaling as much as she could as quickly as the confines of her jaw allowed. Noel took her time, sampling a mouthful here and there, but turning in a complete circle to survey her surroundings.

Perceived freedom.

Tail twitching, Noel was at a crossroads. I could see it in her eyes, that she was fully aware that breaking free from me would grant her unlimited access to the big world around her.

No fences. Trails leading away from her pen. A dirt road just a stone's throw away.

Noel's lower lip twitched in thought. I didn't try to stop her thought process. I stood still, holding the long lunge line in my hand, moving with Belle as she grazed, letting Noel make up her mind.

Another moment or two of circling, head high, neck tense, ears alert, tail twitching, and then Noel joined Belle, dropped her head and grazing.

Content.

We stood in the field for awhile, grazing and breathing, moving methodically forward in a zig-zag, until we found ourselves in a thick grove of tall pines with their lowest branches at least five feet off the ground.

Noel lit up like a little girl in a fairytale. Moving forward at a faster clip, she placed herself in the middle of five closely placed trunks. I let her move to the end of the lunge line, exploring independently. It was the most confident I had seen her move forward.

Noel stopped in the thicket, raising her head high, not out of fear, but out of curiosity. She touched the end of her nose to a snow-covered branch, sniffing gently. Her contact unleashed a small shower of frozen crystals down on her face, and, surprised, she recoiled her nose, shaking her head.

Another moment of magic, and then she rejoined Belle in the open to fill her belly.

Uneventfully, we returned to the bottom of the hill where the safety of fences welcomed us.

With such exciting progress, maybe it was bad timing to be taking a trip to Indianapolis the following weekend, and I regretted the expensive flights I had already booked to make the trip.

It was just a visit home to run around in a big circle. The world-famous Indy Mini Marathon was taking place, and I'd signed up months prior to keep myself accountable and motivate myself to run on a more regular basis.

But I could just run around Colorado and have more time to spend working with Noel.

Too much balance, I chastised myself for the decisions I'd made months prior. *Who needs to spend a weekend at home when you have a wild burro who needs attention?*

May 1, 2018
Colorado Springs, Colorado
Two Years, Nine Months Captive
One Year Rescued
Three Months, Twenty-Eight Days Home

"We're getting another admission."

I groaned. Which nurse was I supposed to assign another fresh surgical patient? The ward was a disaster, everyone was running around trying to finish a long list of tasks, and we were drowning in patients.

Tuesdays were always train wrecks, though. The hospital could never seem to stagger surgeries throughout the week, so the workload on individual weekdays became somewhat predictably overwhelming. Almost every weekend was slow, we would accumulate a few surgical patients on Mondays, and then on Tuesdays, the world would implode, the unit would max out, and nurses wouldn't have time to pee for twelve hours.

I was training to work as a charge nurse. I'd worked under charge nurses often enough to know the generality of the position, but executing the mission was another challenge. I found out really quickly that it wasn't my cup of tea. Given the choice, I'd rather spend my day caring for five patients and managing my own time and tasks than managing six or seven nurses who were attempting to do the same. *Patient care* is why I went back to school for nursing, not staff and resource management, spending a shift wilting behind a computer.

I was crunching numbers and assessing acuity of patients when the house supervisor walked up to the charge nurse station. "I have an admission from the emergency department that you're going to take."

I blinked hard a couple times before I was able to feign a polite grin. "Okay," I said agreeably.

"The patient is intoxicated and suicidal. The patient does not have a safety attendant, but I am mandating that you take the patient anyway."

More blinks, but I wasn't able to plaster a pleasant expression on my face the second time. "That's not how it works. We have a policy that all patients with suicidal ideation have a safety attendant at their bedside."

"I know what your policy is. But I trump your policy."

"No. That's not how it works." All evidence of a fake smile was gone from my face. I could feel the familiar wave of defeat hit me like a ton of bricks. All I wanted to do was come to work and take care of patients, advocate for people who needed me. Instead, every shift resulted in some sort of confrontation and I was always on the losing end.

The house supervisor boasted her authority for a few more minutes, beating me down while I was forced to sit still and take the verbal hits, my eyelids half lowered after the spark faded from my eyes, the dull pressure in my chest that I'd come to experience at some point every time I set foot in the hospital creeping up my sternum. Finally, with her ego boosted, the house supervisor left.

I sighed and pulled my phone out of my pocket while I had a minute to breathe.

But an even more disheartening message awaited me.

Terry has suffered a major heart attack. He's awake and alert at the Heart Hospital downtown.

There was just one uncle in my paternal lineage.

Terry.

Terry had just one nephew, my brother, and one niece.

Me.

I need to get home.

But I was imprisoned, legally bound to the care of patients on the ward until my relief arrived closer to 7:00 P.M. The unit was far from understanding in regards to family crises. Other nurses had told me stories that they'd ask for time off from work to attend funerals or handle major emergencies and been denied the time away, or else requested by management that they find coverage for the shifts they would miss.

An uncle a thousand miles away who had a heart attack but was awake and alert would likely not grant me an early release from my duties.

I had a flight scheduled to leave Denver the following morning. In less than twenty-four hours, I'd be home.

A barrage of communication between my phone and family put me a little more at ease. Terry sounded stable. His heart attack had been massive, and he wasn't expected to recover, but he was resting comfortably in the Heart Hospital, talking, with stable vital signs.

I searched flights home nonetheless. I'd already paid for my flight that was scheduled to leave the next morning, but knew that changing the departure would be an option. Not for cheap, though. Four or five hundred dollars just to land in Indianapolis half a day earlier than my scheduled time.

Did I have fourteen hours to gamble?

It was a toss-up, but the best guess amongst my family was "yes". Terry was stable, for the time being.

I felt a little sick to my stomach thinking of delaying my arrival by more than half a day, but the combination of the insensitive management practices on the ward and the price of changing my flight were major deciding factors.

I had responsibilities that were harder to get away from than a typical job.

How dare I have wondered how a trip to Indiana was going to affect Noel's progress. Five days away could have been the equivalent of being down with the flu, if I'd been so unfortunate. She'd be cared for and fed with a clean pen, and might not even notice my absence.

But cross-country calls and texts don't replace time with family.

Hang in there, Terry.

I knew he, too, was in good hands. His family was at his bedside, he could watch whatever he wanted on TV in his hospital room, and he was in a specialized care setting in a city well-known for excellence in health care. He was okay.

I'll be there soon.

May 2, 2018
Indianapolis, Indiana
Noel's Years Captive: Irrelevant
Noel's Months Rescued: Unimportant
Terry's Days Home: 1

"Terry Tappy, 68, of Greenfield, passed away Wednesday, May 2, 2018 at St. Vincent Heart Hospital in Indianapolis. He was born May 20, 1949 in Huntington, Indiana to Lewis and Marjorie Tappy. Terry enjoyed watching Gunsmoke *and* Walker, Texas Ranger. *He retired from* Shares, Inc. *in Greenfield.*

Terry is survived by his mother, his brother Roger (Lisa) Tappy of Ingalls; niece, Andrea (Joe) Krebsbach; and nephew, Ross (Andrea) Tappy. He was preceded in death by his father.

Per the family's wishes, cremation will take place."

I didn't change my flight.

I wasn't there.

I'm sorry, Terry.

Rest in peace.

May 12, 2018
Black Forest, Colorado
Two Year, Nine Months Captive
One Year Rescued
Four Months, Nine Days Home

I showed up naked, in the way that missing a vital possession made me feel.

I couldn't believe that, in my excitement to leave the house, I'd left my phone behind, on a day when I had most wanted to document my experiences to help remember them in as much detail as possible.

It could have been worse, I thought as I sipped coffee from my travel mug. *I could have shown up uncaffeinated.*

Technically, I'd arrived at the barn an hour early. If I drove home, five miles an hour over the speed limit, and caught mostly green lights, I would only miss the first ten minutes of the clinic.

But I didn't want to miss a single second. I'd been given an invaluable opportunity, thanks to the generosity and forward thinking of the owner of the boarding facility. Her connections through the 4-H Horse and Pony program had brought her a woman organizing a clinic about training longears who needed a place to host the event. She'd offered up the big outdoor arena at her ranch for the entire day in exchange for granting me, her boarder, free admission to the event.

Nervous energy and excitement kept me awake all night. Not only had it been more than ten years since I'd attended a clinic of any kind, I also had never participated in one. A quiet spectator draped over the fence, I always took away new tidbits of invaluable information when I observed clinics. I was ecstatic to find out what kind of new wisdom I would absorb being a participant.

When the first trucks and trailers started rolling up, I knew it was time for the hardest part of the day: getting Noel safely to the arena so that we could participate. I planned on taking Belle along, too, and tying her nearby to the fence to put Noel more at ease.

It went about as well as I'd expected.

Our debut into the arena was accented in a plume of dust as Noel bolted, throwing her weight into the wide Nylon band of her halter and dragging me across the sand.

With other animals already present in the arena, I didn't want her to be loose. I didn't want to let go of the rope. So, I held on, falling to my knees and bracing myself as Noel dragged me for a few yards before I regained my footing.

A great note to start on.

Hello, I'm Andrea, and this is Noel, I mocked myself in my head. *We are both clueless, and she drags me around like this a lot.*

"Why," the clinician started, taking his time verbalizing his expertise into words. "Why… would you not just let go?"

I blinked stupidly. "I don't want her to learn that she can get away from me."

"Learn that she can get away from you!" he scoffed. "She already knows she can get away from you! Hanging onto the end of that rope isn't teaching her anything. Every donkey always knows that they can get away whenever they want to. They are bigger and stronger than any of us. They can get away with no effort at all. You have to make her *want* to obey."

I was hit with my first hard truth of the day. I'd been doing it all wrong. *She has to want to obey. I can't make her.* I committed it to my memory.

I glanced over at Belle, who had calmly accepted being tied in the baking sun along the fence line, unable to eat grass or move to a shadier area. Sweet Belle, a unicorn, content to follow whatever vague direction I half-heartedly gave her, agreeably cooperating with me to facilitate Noel's involvement in the clinic. Sweet Belle, who had been easy to lead from the time that she was an inexperienced yearling. She'd never pulled away from me, never bolted, never wanted to do anything other than behave and please the humans around her. If only I'd been able to thank her in English to sufficiently relay my gratitude for her attitude.

I didn't have long to dwell. Noel was dancing around me unchecked, constantly on the move. Her feet kicked up dust as she shuffled through the sand, her ears rotating east, west, north, then south. Her head swiveled as if hung on a loose hinge, soaking in all of the stimulation that was around her. I willed myself to hone in on what the clinician was teaching, and begin participating.

It wasn't just clinic participation that I avoided, but any situation that put me at the center of attention. I was always an observer, content to stand back and soak in as much information as possible from the sidelines. I didn't like speaking in front of an audience, or letting others in the audience watch me make mistakes and fumble through learning new skills. I was far outside of my comfort zone, dancing with Noel in the middle of a broad arena. I knew all eyes were on us, because we were the most novice, making the most ruckus. It's human nature to struggle looking away from a train wreck.

We were the train wreck that May.

Two choices, I coached myself. *One, revert to a comfortable state of quiet, playing along and not asking questions. Or, two, make a fool of yourself, speak up, try new things, ask the stupid questions, and block the thought of having an audience from your mind.*

My overarching goal was for the clinic to benefit Noel. I needed to learn how to help her. So, I vowed to ask questions, speak up when I needed clarification, and not overanalyze whether we spent the entire day making complete fools of ourselves or not.

My chance to step even more outside of my comfort zone came sooner rather than later. We'd worked fairly extensively on how to move away from pressure on the halter, but no one in the audience could probably tell. Every time I used the lead rope in my hands, Noel's tail flicked in annoyance and she thrust the weight of her body into her head, applying far too much leverage against the rope in my hand for me to have any real control.

I couldn't even get my burro to stand still. How was I going to effectively guide her through an eight-hour-long clinic?

As she shuffled, ignoring me, and I watched all of the other participants effectively completing the tasks that were assigned to them, I knew I'd reached an impasse where I was going to have to make a fool of myself and speak up.

All eyes were already on me, anyway, I was sure. We were the spectacle. The newest donkey owner paired with the burro who'd been in captivity for the shortest amount of time.

We were a mess.

What more was a stupid question piled on top of embarrassing feats of the day?

I fought back my reservations and raised my hand, garnering some one-on-one attention from the clinician. I expressed my concerns.

I thought I'd been able to troubleshoot these types of issues many years earlier, sitting in the stands around much larger arenas, part of far bigger crowds, watching other people struggle around the arena with their project equine. I'd watched a multitude of clinicians work through a wide variety of problems with nervous, flighty, disrespectful, or completely untrained horses. I thought I'd absorbed a small piece of their wisdom each time I sat through a clinic. After all, I'd gotten Belle as a yearling and put her first several rides in her saddle, working through roadblocks, creating a respectful partner who was easy to work alongside.

But Belle was a horse.

Noel was a donkey.

Belle grew up with the finer things in life.

Noel was born a nuisance pest, trapped and then held in captivity without individualized attention.

Belle's bloodline had been honed for generations.

Noel was the result of whatever combination of creatures crossed paths at the right time.

And I was the same human, applying the same techniques that had been so successful for Belle to a feral member of a completely different species.

I deserved whatever judgment was passed on me by the crowd.

I remember struggling to put my questions into words. Ultimately, I wanted to convey, "help, I'm lost, and everything needs to be fixed!" I managed, however, to string together a conglomerate of words to form a sub-intelligible sentence.

"You're telling us to correct our animals when they aren't paying attention to our cues. But, Noel is constantly focused on something else, her feet are constantly moving, and I feel like I'm over-correcting."

"Well, you are."

Good. I needed blunt truthfulness. I needed to embrace being knocked down a peg, needed to regroup, and then needed start back up from a more productive state of mind.

"Okay."

"Relax."

"Relax? But, what do I do when-"

"Relax."

"... Okay, but I feel like I should be-"

"Re. Lax."

I paused longer this time. *Relax?* What exactly did that mean in this context? Relax until Noel moved even further away from me? Relax until she pulled the rope free of my hands and then chase her across the arena? How, exactly, with an untrained, determined, five-hundred-pound animal actively trying to flee the scene was I supposed to relax?

I just was. Relaxation is not an easily learned trait. If it was as easy as hearing a single word for someone to eliminate all external source of stress and anxiety from their consciousness, there would be no market for Xanax. But, the makers of Xanax aren't going out of business anytime soon.

The real issue, then, becomes how to control the emotions of the handler so they don't spill over and affect the decision-making processes of the animal.

But that's an even harder concept to learn in a clinical setting.

I was becoming a flunky right before my own eyes, and I couldn't stop it. I was falling short of grasping the first concept presented in the clinic, the other participants were off to the races, advancing their skill sets and building upon the foundation we were all supposed to have established in the first step.

Next, the clinician directed the handlers in the ring to perform a series of exercises based around the concept of pressure and release. Apply pressure using the rope attached to the halter, release as soon as there is a response.

I'd practiced plenty of that with Noel, and I was happy to pick back up. I was glad to have an exercise to guide Noel through rather than just hoping she would eventually stand still. I picked up the rope and pulled forward, gently.

Noel shifted her weight. I kept applying pressure, waiting for a small step forward.

Again, I was called out.

I was doing it wrong.

"Why are you waiting until she takes a step?" the clinician asked.

"I'm just waiting on her to take one small step, then I'll release pressure."

"A whole step?!"

I paused again, thinking back on my sentence. What had I said that was wrong?

"There's about a hundred little movements this donkey is making before she gets to the point of taking an entire step."

I blinked.

"She moved an ear towards you, she leaned towards you, she shifted her weight onto her opposite legs. You missed all those chances to take the pressure off. Take the pressure off sooner."

Take the pressure off sooner.

I may as well have failed high school physics. Pressure? Remove it? For moving an ear towards me? My relatively-educated brain could barely comprehend the concept in terms that applied to both the animal on the end of my rope and the exercise at hand.

Expect less before letting up, remove the pressure with a smaller response, reward less of a try. My brain offered its most valiant attempt at generating synonyms to help me grasp the exercise.

Take the pressure off.

A step forward wasn't the goal. Not the way I remembered it being the goal when I coached Belle as a yearling. A step is a huge effort. An entire step. Eighteen inches of body move forward to accommodate a full step. An entire leg has to tense its muscles, bend its knee, lift its hoof, propel forward. The animal's entire body has to shift its weight to accommodate. For a split second, standing on three hooves, the animal is vulnerable, more vulnerable than it is when it's rigidly maintaining a standing position.

Take the pressure off sooner.

I'd failed her.

Asking too much, too soon, failing to reward the tiny tries.

I hoped our trainer-burro relationship was reparable.

Take the pressure off sooner.

If anyone had been set up for failure on this component of burro gentling, it was me. I had completely ignored this entire concept in my own life. How, then, could I have expected myself to implement the same concept when working with a wild animal.

I hadn't taken the pressure off myself in some time. It wasn't even within my control to take some of that massive, crushing pressure off my shoulders. Work, in a negative place, for twelve hours straight, never yielding, management expecting more, downtime never an option. It wasn't an excuse, for example, to miss out on updating required training modules because I was too busy caring for patients, so I'd stay late after spending twelve hours caring for patients to finish administrative tasks.

It wasn't acceptable to leave early to fly home to say goodbye to my uncle.

Take the pressure off sooner.

Reward less of an attempt.
Yield more.

I grappled with the philosophy that I was absorbing. Less of a try with less of an ask is more of a success than a bigger, more measurable outcome that required more of an ask to obtain it.

Take the pressure off.

I'm so sorry, Noel, I thought. I was immediately, overwhelming grateful for the grace of a hard-headed animal who held her own and had no qualms about telling me in a big way when I'd pushed it too far.

She's been telling me this whole time.

Take the pressure off.

I worked hard to embrace and apply all of the principles that were presented during the clinic, but continued to beat myself up over my inadequacies as Noel's human.

The only human Noel had. The human who had taken a chance on her, and wanted nothing but the best for her, but who should have admitted her shortcomings far sooner.

Extenuating circumstances. An excuse, but a factor affecting both our lives, nonetheless.

I was broken. Too hard on myself, failing to take the pressure off in time, I'd been crushed under my own expectations. My job had broken me. Enduring an endless chain of jaded managers with their own best interests in mind, my ideas and autonomy had been torched before they ever had a chance for my career to take flight.

Money. I was motivated by money. It sounded hollow out loud, but far more people would do questionable things for more money if the chance arose. I thought I was just taking a job that was going to pad my bank account, but I'd given away far more than I'd earned. Dignity, respect, appreciation- far more than just words on a resume, I'd willingly entered a chamber of doom and sacrificed the quality of my life for the purpose of watching digits slowly add together on my banking apps.

I didn't need the money, not so to speak. I'd have a roof over my head and food on my table with a far smaller paycheck. I'd have food in my dog bowls and hayracks, too. I didn't need nice clothes, didn't need anything with a name brand stamped on it, didn't need a luxury car.

I'd endured pressure, endless pressure, from work and school in the name of advancement with the promise of a bright future.

But I forgot to take the pressure off.

More, and more, and more, and more I'd endured.

I needed a way out. But I was still closed-minded, not able to step far enough back to see the picture in its entirety.

I didn't know at the time that it would be another year before the universe finally would have reacted to the fire that I left kindling under my last nerve and would douse the flames with a cold wake-up.

A sign.

I'd leave my job, take my life back, and start fresh on the other side of the country.

But I didn't know.

I kept scrambling in that arena atop the inferno of sand, asking stupid questions and struggling to pinpoint the perfect time to take the pressure off.

When, the entire time, the right time was now.

Take the pressure off.

Continuing to work through the exercises during the rest of the clinic, the points started driving themselves home more and more. I was learning and committing as much as I possibly could to memory.

There is a theory that the phenomenon of déjà vu is the brain's attempt to actively create a memory from events occurring in the present. Remembering such a theory, I tried to concentrate on replicating the sensation of déjà vu. I wanted to formulate the memory of what I was learning before the clinic had even ended.

I never felt the unsettling stir of false recollection wash over my conscious, but I did a sufficient job of remembering moments with such detail that I can still look at the pictures in my mind's eye. I can still remember the incredible change in Noel's demeanor from the start of the clinic to the end.

Driving home, I was overwhelmed.

Overwhelmed by hope, humility, and amazement at the intellect of the burro I had adopted.

Procrastinating from doing my homework that evening, I pulled up a blank document and typed everything I could remember from the clinic. Pulling that document up on my computer screen fabricated another digitally stamped memory that I could open whenever I needed a refresher:

Breathe. Relax. She can tell when I'm tense even if I think I'm wearing a poker face.
Do not pull on Noel's head with static pressure. Use dynamic energy when asking Noel to do something. For example, if she won't walk, rather than pulling on the rope in one direction and waiting for Noel to respond, change the pressure by pulling side to side.

When Noel tries to pull away, don't pull back to try to stop her. She knows she can get away. I'm not teaching her anything by trying to fight it. There are two things I can try when she tries to get away: First, if I have enough slack, bump her head towards me hard by yanking all the slack out of the rope rapidly. But, do not try to apply steady pressure. I will lose that fight every time.

Second, if there is not enough slack to create an effective bump, or if the first maneuver doesn't work, let her go. Throw the rope at her. Let her leave. She won't try as hard to get away if she's not fighting to escape from anything. (I was shocked that this technique was immediately effective at thwarting her escape efforts).

THINK SMALLER.

May 13, 2018
Colorado Springs, Colorado
Two Year, Nine Months Captive
One Year Rescued
Four Months, Ten Days Home

     I brewed a pot of coffee the next morning, awake in time to catch the short window of morning during which the rising sun casts an incredible pink glow over the front range. Audrey joined me on the back porch while I sipped my first mug of coffee, lying at my feet while I pondered the hours of information I'd absorbed the day before.

     I'd acquired a deep sunburn, having been so focused on the present, for once, that I didn't feel the effects of the sun and hadn't thought to bring sunscreen or a long-sleeved shirt to shield myself from the rays. I felt the aftermath of my exposure, both reflected in the sun and the new perspectives dancing in my head.

Having captured the essence of communication with Noel and new, relationship-enhancing exercises to perform in the notes I'd jotted the night before, I had committed the important takeaways to a permanent record. However, another piece of wisdom that had rolled off the tongue of the clinician had struck me in such a way that I hadn't written it down for two reasons. First, the simple appearance of seven words at the end of the outline would not have come close to capturing the chain of thoughts that they triggered for me in the hot sun. Second, I had a feeling I wouldn't forget what had been said.

Don't treat her like a wild animal.

The sentence was more straightforward than the abstract-to-me concept of trying to simultaneously relax, concentrate hard enough to read extremely subtle cues in Noel's body language, respond to them only sometimes, and other times ignore them and wait for an opportunity to provide positive reinforcement. Similar to the field of nursing, information and strategies can be described in words and committed to a piece of paper, but learning how to apply all of the right interventions at the right times without upsetting the patients or their family members was an art form that had to be honed with years of experience.

I was a better nurse in 2018 than I had been as a new grad three years earlier. I would get there with Noel. I just had to take the time to ameliorate my craft.

Don't treat her like a wild animal.

Seemingly more black and white than most of the other advice I'd soaked up. No analysis needed, just "don't do that anymore."

So, leave it to my ever-churning, overactive mind to dissect the words and wonder how true they should ring in my practice with Noel.

Was Noel at the point where it was more beneficial to think of her as an everyday donkey who hadn't grown up in a government holding facility? How would she benefit from me disregarding that very recent history in her life? Was it really having a negative impact on her progress to keep her past as a wild burro at the forefront of my mind?

The pink alpenglow was already beginning to fade into gold. The front range was coming to life. Each crevice and tree line stood prominent against the rocky face, the antennae atop Cheyenne Mountain tickling the blue sky. Bright white snow still capped Pike's Peak, and for an even shorter window of time than the mountains stayed painted pink, the sunlight sometimes illuminated the windows on the visitor's center and created a pinpoint of vivid luminescence flickering otherworldly from 14,115 feet above sea level.

I felt grounded next to the mountains. Massive and solid, the chiseled walls provided a backdrop to reflect the constant metamorphosis of the environment around them. Gray and sleeping before the sun peeked over the Eastern plains, then pink, then gold, then green and full of life. Whitewashed in the winter when heavy clouds shrouded the uppermost peaks from visibility down on the ground. Silver and misty on warmer days when rolling pressure systems brought rain to the front range. Scarred, here and there, from mining activity and damaging wildfires. Beautiful from every angle and each perspective.

Grounded, because the mountains never yielded. Not extreme weather nor a man's ego nor societal conflict could change their bones. Their skin, sure, can wax and wane, topsoil can shift, trees can die, and new trees grow. Snow falls, snow melts. Tourists come, and tourists leave. But the mountains still wake up every morning draped in pink, then gold, then green, ceaselessly.

The life congregating at the base of the peaks, though, was quite the opposite. Cyclically, seasonally, living souls changed. With life spans lasting a fraction of the amount of time that mountains preside, perhaps animal life is just a microcosm of what the mountains eventually experience over eons. I won't live long enough to test that theory, and I can't fathom the magnitude of such an assertion. My perspective, small-minded in comparison to the vast timelessness of the Rocky Mountains, sees living, breathing souls as ever-changing entities in constant flux.

Audrey awoke at my feet, raising her head to twitch her nose in response to the cool morning breeze. Just six years old, her unique silvery coat had made her appear more mature than her tricolor beagle counterpart since the time they were young. She'd changed significantly over the six years that we'd had her, growing from a ferocious puppy who, weighing in at twenty pounds, had destroyed my parents' couch, an entire bed of tulips, and countless pairs of shoes. She'd lived in three states, and had the chance to pee on bushes in seven states. Audrey and Max both were better travelled than some humans. She'd started her life discarded at an animal shelter, but found her Forever Home with us at just three months of age. Audrey's experiences in the world had surely shaped her attitude and level of maturation, and she'd changed for the better.

Max hadn't joined us on the porch for sunrise coffee because he was still in bed. Beagles are commonly used as hunting dogs, but the level of energy and training required for a beagle to succeed in the woods with a hunter had somehow eluded Max. More content to spend his days on the couch or in bed, Max could only be persuaded to move his feet if snacks were involved.

Admittedly, I coddled Max. He, too, had suffered a less-than-desirable start to his life, even more so than Audrey. On a cold January day in Indiana, there were already six inches of snow on the ground when we saw a spray-painted sign in a yard advertising a "free beagle." A short conversation with the owner of the beagle revealed that he lived on a chain in the yard because he destroyed everything in reach, barked constantly, wasn't housebroken, and had some aggressive tendencies- he'd recently bitten a bicyclist who stopped to pet him.

None of it was relevant on that winter day. I was going to give him a home.

According to the man who owned him, the little beagle was so crazed that he shouldn't even be trusted in my car because he would likely destroy the interior. So, the man delivered him to my house in his truck to prevent the beagle from throwing a fit. He came with a collar and a chain, and I was advised to never let Max loose in the yard without also having the chain attached to his collar, because he would undoubtedly dig under the fence and run away.

I nodded my thanks for the advice, and took Max inside.

He tried to pee one time on the floor. I reprimanded him, and he never did it again. Housebroken in an hour, a far cry from the feral creature who had been advertised to me. I let him sleep in my bed that same night, and saw him let out the biggest sigh imaginable when he curled up on a corner of the comforter. His first night's sleep in a heated home on a clean, warm blanket.

He never destroyed or even chewed on anything, including his toys. His idea of playing was to gently carry around stuffed animals with the tips of his teeth so as not to harm them.

I threw the chain away.

Not only did Max never even attempt to dig under the fence, it seemed like he didn't even know how to use the infamous "beagle nose" that tends to get some hounds lost on endless trails. He would panic if he got too far away from me and run to close the gap. After proving his loyalty and good behavior for a couple of years, he didn't even need a leash on long hikes. He didn't want to leave us.

I always kept his underprivileged beginning close to memory, and tried to pamper Max every chance I found to make up for the year spent in the cold on a chain. Max was allowed to sleep on as many blankets as he wanted, got belly rubs whenever he asked, and always got handouts from my dinner plate.

I supposed Max's start in life did shape the way I perceived him. But had it affected the way he assimilated into a middle class home in a neighborhood? He was such a good boy- had it had any kind of negative impact?

Audrey had been "rescued" too, yet I didn't think of her start the same way as Max's. She'd been delivered to a climate-controlled animal shelter as a puppy and came home when she was three months old- not anywhere near fully mature. I would be surprised if she even remembered her time behind bars.

As Audrey jumped onto my lap, digging her elbows into my thighs in her pursuit of a comfortable place to lie down while I finished my first cup of coffee, I wondered how long the title of "rescued" is supposed to stick with animal who ends up in a good home. A day? A year? A lifetime? Did it matter? Was it relevant to either of their stories that Audrey was a quarter of Max's age when she was rescued?

The same answerless questions applied to scenarios with more negative connotations, too, I mulled. People addicted to substances earned the societal titles of "users" or "addicts." Is there any relevance to the number of months or years that a person uses drugs or alcohol in terms of applying the label to them? Is there any amount of time that an addict can spend without abusing any substances to erase the designation from their repertoire? Even at Alcoholics Anonymous and Narcotics Anonymous meetings, participants introduce themselves as addicts who are in perpetual recovery versus completely transformed individuals whose addictions have no further bearing on their lives.

Addiction is subjective. How people feel, how addiction affects their choices, the force that drive the ways they behave when drunk or high, all differ and are not measurable. Alternatively, a public stigma such as obesity has a measurable and objective definition, easily referenced in a chart categorizing body-mass indices.

The state of living in the wild is certainly objective. Human eyes can see an untamed, unbranded burro roaming the sandy hills in the West. The label "wild," though, was far less objective when applied to a burro living at an upscale boarding facility, branded, able to be touched and haltered.

At what point was my wild burro no longer a wild burro? The minute she and her mother entered the trap at the Chemehuevi Reservation? Upon arrival to a holding facility, or after being taken into the rescue? The day a human hand touched her for the first time?

Or, like an addict, was "wild" always a label that would follow her, having permanently affected the way she processes the world and reacts to new situations?

My train of thought changed gears, like it was staggering up the steep incline on the Manitou Cog Railway, destined for the peak that stood proudly before me. The golden hue of Pike's Peak had transitioned to yellow as the sun climbed higher in the sky, and the wide groves of pine were more recognizable, dark green, halting abruptly where the level of elevation approached 10,000 feet and gave way to barren red rocks.

Don't treat her like a wild animal.

Why?

Was it affecting Noel's psyche to view her as a wild animal in captivity rather than a domestic donkey? Noel was smart, incredibly so, but she couldn't read my mind. I never greeted her, "hello, wild burro." I never stopped her from exploring or learning something new with the admonishment, "hey, you're a wild animal, you can't act domestic."

What about this sentence, then, was so important?

It hit me the way a bomb cyclone hit the Pike's Peak region in the winter, suddenly, freezing me in my place. As much as I wanted it to be about her, as much easier as it would make the entire process if donkey training was all about Noel, it was about me. It all circled back to me. Me, who hates being the center of attention. The journey of gentling refers to the animal, but also centers on the human driving the process forward.

I'd spent Saturday at the clinic being told to relax when I didn't realize I appeared so tense. I required near-constant reminders to breathe and to stop moving my own body to accommodate Noel's movements. I spent the day focused on Noel, on helping her, but it all came back to me. Me, as her leader. I needed to deeply understand and control myself before I could help her learn to do the same.

How, then, would thinking of Noel as a wild burro differ from perceiving her as a domestic-but-untrained equine?

Vastly.

I thought back to Belle, yearling Belle. An animal who grew up with every advantage a horse could dream about, she progressed so quickly. I was confident working with her. I hauled her to an open horse show in a neighboring county two days after I took her home from the Indiana State Fair for the first time. Belle stood tied to the trailer next to another young, but domestic, horse. We entered two classes, and I was proud to parade her before the judges. We took home ribbons. Two days after I met her.

I was confident, I repeated to myself again.

Four months and ten days after she came home, I still anticipated Noel to act out like a wild burro. My perception didn't shape Noel at all, but my perception shaped my own body language greatly, setting off a chain reaction that would affect her in the end.

Titles aren't a handicap until we make them into a handicap, like I'd subconsciously done to Noel.

I needed to change.

May 15, 2018
Black Forest, Colorado
Two Years, Nine Months Captive
One Year Rescued
Four Months, Twelve Days Home

Enlightenment: the phenomenon I thought I'd experienced after my mind was opened at the clinic on Saturday.

I had applied some of the principles that I'd learned, and dressed Noel in a rope halter for more leverage. I was confident, or so I told myself. My donkey was going to have her first farrier appointment.

Metaphorically, there were more heavy-duty tools in my resource belt, but I walked lighter. More tools meant more answers, more progress, and more understanding. I was on the right track.

I was capable. I had hands and eyeballs, seemingly the two most important prerequisites for reading the fine print on my burro's brain.

But, as it turned out, I was still doing everything wrong.

"That clinician and I do things just a little bit differently," the farrier explained gently. "A Nylon halter would be just fine."

I recalled one of my main takeaways from the clinic had been to start applying a rope halter to increase my leverage and teach Noel to be more responsive, and I was reminded of the reason why so many different equine clinicians present their techniques. There is no singular "right" way to do things. There is no singular "push this button to solve all your problems" in the equine industry. It was true of horses, so, by default, it must be even more true of their longer-eared counterparts.

I'd seen impressive results during the clinic, and I proceeded to be blown away, again, by what the farrier was able to accomplish in just twenty minutes.

I'd demonstrated the technique I'd been using to lift Noel's feet, wrapping the rope around a foot and pulling gently until it lifted off the ground.

However, just minutes later, the farrier was gently cueing Noel to take her weight off her legs with his hands, no extra ropes required.

I got another lesson in relaxation, driving the point home that I hadn't fully mastered my body language nor my confidence in the three short days since we participated in the clinic. We weren't able to trim Noel that day- I hadn't prepared her well enough- but we made an appointment for the first official trim, and I was able to make another outline of points to remember.

Two polar opposite training styles, two different personalities, but the same impressive effect on Noel: progress. I realized the two most important prerequisites have nothing to do with the presence of eyeballs or hands. Rather, calling upon industry experts, realizing and trying to understand my own shortcomings, and staying as open-minded as possible to keep learning were the gating factors.

Finishing my outline of things learned from our new farrier rather than finishing a lengthy research paper, I took the first bullet point quite literally, and rolled out my yoga mat.

I was determined to help Noel, and first I had to help myself.

Another night of procrastination generated another outline of reminders I needed to keep at the forefront of my mind.

Namaste. Seriously, RELAX.
I can condition myself to relax in scenarios where I would usually become tense: Forced laughter during times of stress eventually becomes innate calmness during situations which used to cause tension.
Be respectful by picking her foot up and putting it down as if it is very fragile.
Press forward at the joint to ask her to take the weight off her leg
Always have Noel on rope when beginning this so that I can apply and release pressure without her running away.

June 2, 2018
Black Forest, Colorado
Two Years, Ten Months Captive
One Year, One Month Rescued
Four Months, Thirty Days Home

In Colorado, sometimes the weather outside the front door was different than the weather outside the back door. Sunny and warm one direction, whiteout snowstorm in the other.

Similarly, it seemed, the emotional climate out the back gate of the paddock is a far cry from that of the front gate.

"Easy, easy, easy," I coached, tugging backwards on the ropes in my hands.

Normally mellow and placid, Belle was excited to reach the fresh green grass beckoning from the front pasture, and her energy fueled Noel, who pranced alongside me.

It might have seemed a bit far-fetched to attempt a stroll out front to the big pasture. Out front, where cars and dogs could show up at any given moment. A pasture encircled by sagging cable, loose enough for Noel to crawl through or even short enough for a hop over the top. An area where we might again find ourselves being a spectacle, with lots of potential observers. We'd be closer to a busy road than we'd ever been before, too.

Namaste, namaste, namaste, I snapped at myself internally.

I was just taking my donkey and my horse out to eat some grass. I wanted to give Noel the opportunities to figure out how to live her best life at a horse barn, and she wasn't going to figure it out if we stuck to places out back where we felt comfortable.

So, I pushed us out of our comfort zone while trying to stay as relaxed as possible.

An oxymoron from every perspective.

We worked through a few balks, overcame a desire to rush to the front pasture as fast as our little legs would allow, steered away from the driveway that led straight to the busy road, and made it to the pasture.

We did it. I remember being a little disappointed in the level of my surprise.

Breathe, breathe, breathe. Namaste, namaste, namaste.

Belle and Noel's hard work at walking through a new section of the ranch without any major train wrecks was rewarded with a huge field of green grass to graze. Then their happy state of being rewarded me in return when they picked their heads up and stretched their legs, enjoying the wide open space and the chance to just be equine for an afternoon. My smile stretched ear to ear when Belle galloped past me several times in big circles, her tail flying, and Noel put her best feet forward in an attempt to keep up. She looked so happy, flying faster than I'd ever seen her, smartly cutting corners to gallop in a smaller circle than Belle.

Never once did Noel steer herself towards the low points in the fence, attempt an escape, or even evade capture when it was time to put them back in their pen. If she took the time to size up a potential escape under the fence line, she never executed.

The three of us walked back to their pen in a far more positive state of mind than we'd started out, and I was too proud of the accomplishment to hide my expression.

Point taken. My donkey had made enormous strides at adapting to her new life, in spite of the barriers I kept throwing up with my own imperfections as her leader.

What a blessing to experience grace from an animal four times my size, who didn't have to listen to me if she didn't want to.

She was choosing to be my partner.

June 20, 2018
Black Forest, Colorado
Two Years, Ten Months Captive
One Year, One Month Rescued
Five Months, Seventeen Days Home

I felt weightless, so filled with joy to see the first hoof trimming drop silently onto the soft sand.

The single event I'd been the most nervous about when Noel came home, Hoof Trimming Day, was underway. She wasn't happy about it, but she was allowing it to happen. Her hooves were being trimmed and shaped, like a real domestic donkey.

Sheepishly, I thought of the tools that were hidden in the trunk of my car- hoof nippers and a rasp that I'd ordered on Amazon during the phase when I feared I'd never be able to trust Noel to stand for a farrier, nor that I'd find a farrier willing to trim a wild burro.

I met every other barrier I'd encountered in my life with an attitude of "I'll just do it myself." I didn't like asking for help, and felt uncomfortable when other people did favors for me. My freshman year at Purdue, I'd wanted to rearrange my dorm room, and tried to adjust the height of my lofted bed. I'd ended up dropping the bed from its lofted height of five feet straight onto the floor, creating a deafening crash. Rather than ask for help or even explain the situation I'd found myself in, I hid when the residents from the floor below me had knocked on my door to find out what had caused the apocalyptic bang.

So, I had the idea that I could apply that same attitude to Noel's hoof health, and learn how to do it myself. I ordered the tools I would need, watched YouTube videos, and even considered cashing in a couple weeks of vacation time at work to attend a farrier course in Wyoming. Thankfully, I hadn't found the time to sign up for that class.

Watching the farrier examine angles and expertly shape Noel's hooves, I was relieved that I hadn't attempted to tackle the task myself. There were at least a dozen ways it could have ended in disaster if I took a sharp hoof nipper to Noel's foot without knowing what I was doing.

A sense of independence and a can-do attitude are important, but it's just as necessary to know when to step back and rely on experts. Watching Noel's last hoof rest back on the ground with a beautiful, shiny rounded toe, I could feel my face light up.

I was thankful I'd taken the leap and trusted myself to tackle the project of gentling Noel because it offered unparalleled feelings of success and joy like these. But I was also proud of myself for entrusting the community to help out in ways that their expertise best facilitated Noel's health and progress.

It takes a village.

July 4, 2018
Colorado Springs, Colorado
Two Years, Eleven Months Captive
One Year, Two Month Rescued
Six Months, One Day Home

    They'd arrived- the only products I've ever ordered with the hope that they would just sit somewhere collecting dust, never needing to be used.

    They were fluorescent orange, heavy-duty Velcro straps, and my name and number embroidered in thick, black threading. Water-resistant plastic sleeves with a thick piece of paper for writing additional notes. Sixty dollars for the two of them, not including shipping.

    Evacuation collars.

    In a perfect world, wildfires would serve their natural purpose of eradicating dense underbrush from forests and allowing new growth, out in the middle of nowhere, never affecting structures or cities. In a less-perfect-but-still-one-of-the-better-case-scenarios, wildfires threatening the ranch would give humans plenty of warning, and we'd have time to drive to the barn, load the animals and supplies, and haul our precious hooved friends to a safe place until the threat to their safety was gone.

    Unfortunately, that's not how it works all the time. The burn scars in Black Forest and nearby Waldo Canyon were humbling reminders of the devastating potential of wildfires and the speed at which they can grow with little warning for anyone to evacuate.

In the event that a wildfire started threatening the animals at the ranch, the equine would simply be turned loose to find their own way to safety, and we would cross all of our fingers and toes that we would be able to locate them after it was extinguished. It was one time where I knew Noel would be an excellent role model for Belle to follow. Her instincts had evolved to keep her safe, and she was still very aware and critical of any situation which could threaten her safety. I knew, if the time ever came, she'd bolt towards safety, and Belle would likely follow.

If left to her own devices, I knew that Belle would revert to her own domestic Quarter Horse logic and would likely keep trying to return to the place where she knows she's always been safe, happy, and fed- the barn. In fact, it's a common way for horses to perish in fires. They have an instinct to survive just like any other mammal, but their logic is flawed, likely influenced by many generations of captive horses that didn't have to think too critically about how to keep from dying. In captivity, humans have accounted for all of those problems, giving horses safe paddocks, regular feedings, and strong leadership.

All the horses are doing is trying to return to that safety net that they know exists at the barn.

"If you ever have to wear this and get turned loose, run, really fast and really far," I lectured Noel. "Belle will follow you. Just go east. Keep running east away from all these trees, and I'll meet you under the windmills, okay?"

Noel pressed her head into me, asking for an ear rub. I obliged.

"Let's make sure they fit."

I strapped the first collar around Belle's neck. A gorgeous, dark seal bay, fluorescent safety orange was not her most flattering accent color. But it stood out, and my phone number was very easily visible. I wanted to make sure a good Samaritan could see the number from afar without having to actually approach the animals, a feature which, of course, cost even more money to embroider onto the collars. Belle was a puppy dog, but she'd never survived a natural disaster, and I wasn't sure how traumatized she may be, or how much she may be influenced by Noel's standoffish demeanor in a survival situation. I wanted to ensure that all of the most important information would be visible from several yards away. Then, on Belle's collar, I included more detailed information on the card inside the plastic sleeve: Belle's and Noel's names and additional points of contact.

"It'll work," I said.

Belle sniffed my pockets.

"Your turn." I turned towards Noel with her collar. She stood still with a bemused look on her face while I attached the collar to her neck. It was hard to determine what size to buy for her unique body type. Some yearling-sized horse equipment fit, some cob-sized horse equipment worked. I was thankful that the pony-sized collar fit well, or I would have been tossing some more money at the company who made her first collar.

"You look beautiful."

Noel's tail twitched.

"Okay, I'll take it off, I just wanted to make sure it fit."

I started peeling the Velcro off itself, and Noel bug-eyed and fled at the sound.

I'd have dropped my face into my hands if they weren't covered in dirt, manure, and fly spray. I hadn't conditioned Noel to the sound of Velcro, and now some of the heaviest-duty Velcro on the market was strapped to her head directly behind her ears. Why had I even attached it? Why hadn't I just wrapped it around her neck, saw that it fit, and went on with my life?

Too late for the what-ifs, I applied everything I'd learned and devised a plan based around positive reinforcement.

First, relax.

Second, breathe.

Third, since I'd scared her with the sound, I'd have to start small, really small. Just a touch of the collar, then a small bite of a cookie. Then a small tug at the collar, and a cookie. Then peeling back just a millimeter of the collar, and another cookie.

It was dusk by the time I removed the collar from Noel's neck. But, it was off, Noel was unscathed, and we both were calm, although Noel's belly was fuller of cookies than mine.

"I've got to go to our neighborhood cookout," I explained, giving Noel one last ear rub. No one would bat an eye that I was late due to my animals. Between work, grad school, and the animals, I rarely spent any waking hours socializing. But I was starving.

And the lesson was over.

Time to take the pressure off.

July 18, 2018
Black Forest, Colorado
Two Years, Eleven Months Captive
One Year, Two Month Rescued
Six Months, Fifteen Days Home

Hmm.

I shook the bottle fly spray, unscrewed the top to look inside and smell the contents, to make sure that the bottle was still filled with potent fly spray. Potent citronella and other mystery chemicals met my nose. It was.

It was the same product that I had been using on Belle. Belle looked fine. The occasional fly would land on her skin, she would twitch, and it would fly away. Save the occasional horsefly, there weren't any insects that were drawing blood on her legs.

I looked back at Noel. There were dozens of pinpoint specks of dried blood clustered around her knees and pasterns. I had been proud that I got her to a point where she would stand to accept the fly spray landing on the sensitive parts of her legs. She hated seeing the fly spray bottle come out, but I was able to get the job done.

I had been told that Noel was so smart that she would soon figure out the fly spray bottle gives her some relief from the flies. But if the fly spray wasn't actually doing its job to repel any insects, and she was enduring painful bites that drew blood, I wasn't sure how she was supposed to associate the fly spray bottle as a friend rather than foe.

I was at a loss. Same product, two different species, two different results.

What else could I do to protect Noel's legs?

I drew on my nursing experience. In the clinical setting in regards to people medicine, Western interventions can generally be grouped into one of two categories: chemical or physical.

For example, in regards to combative psychiatric patients, restraints can come in the flavor of chemicals, such as heavy doses of sedatives and antipsychotics, or they can be physical in nature, such as cotton restraints securing a patient's arms to the bed rails to prevent the patient from harming himself.

Contraceptives fit into the same two categories. Hormonal birth control utilizes chemicals to prevent pregnancy, whereas condoms are a physical barrier.

If chemical fly repellent was not doing the trick, perhaps a physical barrier between Noel's skin and the pests would provide more relief.

I jumped on Google at the barn, although my service wasn't the best, and I found a specific type of fly boot that is made just for donkey legs. Better yet, they came in a purple plaid pattern. Noel's color.

In the meantime, I was not going to let her suffer for seven days until her boots arrived. Wracking my brain, wondering what else I could put on her legs, I decided to take a trip to Big R Farm and Feed down the street, which yielded a haul that I hoped would help- six rolls of self-adhesive vet wrap.

I wasn't even sure how willing Noel would be to let me wrap her legs. I had never put anything on her legs. I wondered if we were in for a rodeo trying to apply the wraps.

I pulled a two-foot-long strip of the vet wrap off the roll, and tucked it into a bucket in the middle of her pen. I put her halter on and then approached her slowly with the wrap. Having learned my lesson after the evacuation collar mishap, I was doing a better job of progressing more slowly, and breaking a task that I used to think as of as a single event into ten or twelve even smaller steps. Small bites were easier for her to chew.

I had a strategy before I simply wrapped the bandage around her legs. I planned to introduce Noel to the bandage, letting her see and smell it, then place the bandage briefly on her skin so she could feel the texture, slowly increasing the intervals of time that I held it against her until she was comfortable with the process.

She hadn't liked the sound of the self-adhesive wrap. But, much to my surprise, she had no qualms about the bandage coming near her. I was noticing a trend, the more time I spent preparing for a new task, the better she seemed to respond to it.

Did that say more about her development, or the state of my psyche?

She didn't even flinch when I secured the adhesive bandage around her legs. I was glad to have some kind of a solution in the works.

Of course, in the days that followed, I would find the bandages trampled into the dirt somewhere in her pen.

Even duct tape wouldn't hold the bandages on.

I'd have to find another solution.

July 20, 2018
Black Forest, Colorado
Two Years, Eleven Months Captive
One Year, Two Month Rescued
Six Months, Seventeen Days Home

    My sixty-dollar purchase landed on my doorstep.

    Noel watched me curiously as I unwrapped a full set of purple plaid fly boots. Having worked through her aversion to the sound of Velcro, I was able to undo the hook-and-loop fasteners without scaring her away.

    She looked fancy with all her legs dressed in purple plaid.

    "I hope these work for you, my girl." I hugged her neck.

    My hope was short-lived. Just a number of hours later, Noel learned how Velcro works. Using her teeth, she was able to grasp the edge of the Velcro straps and undo them, freeing her legs from the boots.

    The next time I came to the barn, I found her boots scattered around her pen, trampled into the mud.

    Point taken.

    Back to the drawing board.

July 30, 2018
Black Forest, Colorado
Two Years, Eleven Months Captive
One Year, Two Month Rescued
Six Months, Twenty-Seven Days Home

The neck of a tiny two-week-old foal is much smaller than the neck of a mature adult burro. Noel's three-year-old brand was barely legible, having stretched and malformed as her body grew underneath it.

I was nervous. What if the brand inspector wasn't convinced that this was the same animal that appeared on the paperwork? What if I wasn't able to obtain the title that would legally make Noel mine?

It was an odd concept for me to grasp. Wild burros and mustangs still belong to the Bureau of Land Management for the first year after they are adopted into a home. Even though I'd been housing, training, and caring for Noel for several months, she wasn't officially mine yet.

It was unnerving to wonder what would happen if something went wrong in the process.

What if she was taken away from me?

I was prepared when the brand inspector arrived. He'd been difficult to get hold of, so I didn't want any more hiccups when he arrived. I had Noel haltered, I had a check ready to write, and I had clippers at the ready in case I needed to (attempt to) clip the longer hairs on her neck to increase the visibility of the brand.

Of all the things about adopting a wild burro that had been ten times more difficult than I expected, the brand inspection went off without a hitch. I wasn't convinced he'd even had time to look at Noel based on the amount of time he spent in the barnyard.

"Yep," he said when he was still fifteen yards from the paddock, then he spun on his heels and walked back to the truck.

I followed. "That's it? She's mine?"

"Yep. That'll be seventy-five dollars."

I happily wrote the check and received the title of my new "wild horse or burro." Wild horse *or* burro? They couldn't even specify? It was as disappointing as when I received my degree after nursing school and realizing it just generally refered to an "Associate's degree in Science." The word "nursing" wasn't even on it.

Just a piece of paper. Just a formality.

But it made Noel mine.

August 1, 2018
Black Forest, Colorado
Two Years, Eleven Months Captive
One Year, Three Months Rescued
Six Months, Twenty-Nine Days Home

Noel's third birthday called for carrots and cookies.

A thousand days of life, and she was still a baby. A three year old horse is often mature enough to wear a saddle around, and start learning how to carry a rider. A three-year-old burro, on the other hand, still acts like a juvenile.

I'd read in some sources that donkeys start to mellow around age six.

Halfway there, we were still learning and progressing every day.

One foot after the other.

"Here's to many more birthdays together, girl."

Crunch, crunch, crunch.

August 12, 2018
Black Forest, Colorado
Two Years, Eleven Months Captive
One Year, Three Months Rescued
Seven Months, Nine Days Home

August had suddenly become our most celebrated month. Less than two weeks later, we were reveling again.

Fourteen years.

Enough time for a human to be conceived, born, and mature into a teenager. Long enough for a fine whiskey to age. Longer than it takes an undergrad to become a doctor.

Countless life events can unfold in fourteen years. In that amount of time, a girl could graduate from high school, get her first job, fall in love, get her first apartment, break up with her first love, graduate college, start a career, hate it, fall in love again, get married, leave the first career, move to another state, go back to school, graduate with a second degree, move to a third state, start a second career, love it, and start graduate school.

And I did.

On our fourteenth anniversary, standing with a bouquet of carrots under the Colorado sun, it was inconceivable that it had been so many years since Belle came home with me for the first time as a yearling.

Even so young and immature, she had always had the best mind sitting between her small ears. Small ears that, once upon a time, had been mocked for their mule-like qualities. One of the unexpected benefits of adopting a burro for Belle was the fact that Noel's long ears made Belle's Quarter Horse ears appear infinitely smaller and more appropriately proportioned.

When she became mine, I hadn't even heard my name announced.

Belle was the subject of the 2004 Indiana Quarter Horse Association 4-H Horse Award presentation. Until 2017, there was a yearling Quarter Horse given away every year at the Indiana State Fair to a 4-H Horse and Pony member. To qualify, interested 4-Hers just needed to submit their answers in essay format to ten questions posed regarding horse training and management. From those essays, ten finalists came to the Indiana State Fair on a designated day to interview with a panel of experts in the equine industry. Based on the combination of essays and interview answers, a 4-H participant took the yearling home the same day.

In 2004, I was fifteen. With only a few years of experience riding horses, I was leasing and borrowing animals to take to the 4-H horse show, and learning more every day. My mom had let me skip school on a couple different occasions to sit at horse training clinics, where I did my best to soak in every scrap of knowledge I could.

I wanted my own horse, and I'd proposed it in a number of ways. I'd asked, I'd hinted, I'd tried working very hard to care for the horses I leased to prove that I was capable.

"No."

The same answer hit me every time the topic arose. A word that can't be connoted as anything other than negative, it only served as motivation for me.

Yes, I will. I was more determined every time I heard it.

A gift from the universe appeared in my hands out of the blue one evening. I spent a lot of evening at the Hancock County Fairgrounds, but Monday nights were devoted to dog obedience training.

I was in the multipurpose indoor arena, the same building that hosted cattle, hogs, sheep, goats, and llamas, with Scruffie. She was ten years old by the time I had invested seven years in my 4-H Dog Obedience project. I had accepted the fact that she wasn't ever going to compete in the same way as a Border collie or a German shepherd. More Lhasa Apso than any other breed, she was best equipped for a lazy walk and a soft blanket, but she loved spending time with her humans. So, we kept showing up to 4-H Dog Obedience practice, spending time together and accepting our recurrently mediocre performances for what they were.

By default, we'd entered the most advanced classes offered in the 4-H program, not by merit, but by years spent enrolling in the program as a team. The advanced classes required an attempt for dogs to search and retrieve a specific target based on scent. At the show, a collection of six identical dumbbells would be placed in front of Scruffie, and she would be required to sniff out the single item that I had personally touched and placed among the group.

Scruffie didn't even want to put the dumbbell in her mouth, let alone find and retrieve a specific dumbbell from a cluster of them.

The dog obedience leader offered suggestions based on techniques that worked for his German shepherds. "It's called the ear pinch method," he coached me. "Just squeeze her ear until she opens her mouth so you can place the dumbbell in her mouth."

A little nauseated before I'd even begun, I stayed open-minded and gave the technique a try, placing the flesh of Scruffie's ear between my fingers and beginning to squeeze. I increased the pressure until she began to wince, then a yelp started to sound from her throat as her jaw opened to accommodate the verbal protest.

"There!" the dog obedience leader affirmed, at the same time that I released all pressure and dropped the dumbbell to the ground.

"I'm not doing that," I asserted.

"It's just a technique to train her to perform the task-"

"I'd rather just take last place."

So, every Monday night, Scruffie and I showed up to spend time together. But, despite being the senior-most team, we failed to progress. During the "long sit" test when the trained obedience dogs are supposed to sit still and upright for three minutes without moving even while their handlers are out of sight, Scruffie usually laid down in a more comfortable position as soon as I stepped out of the ring. I didn't reprimand her, instead enjoying a three-minute break in a back room on a soiled old couch, and allowing Scruffie to take a short nap. During the dumbbell test, she continued to sniff the remnants of livestock that practiced in the same building, ignoring the actual task at hand. I allowed it.

We weren't there to win, but we kept showing up.

A fateful Monday night in early June of 2004, however, a 4-H leader from the administrative building found me in Dog Obedience practice and gifted me a life-changing passport.

"I just wanted to walk this over to you because it's due tomorrow," she said. "It's the application for the Indiana Quarter Horse 4-H Horse Award."

I mustered a, "thank you," taken aback by the time limit. Even at fifteen, I liked to devote time to important tasks. Homework was a chore that could be completed in a single evening, but something as important as an essay application to win a horse was another undertaking.

I spent all evening on it, writing and rewriting my responses. I had excellent handwriting even when I didn't concentrate so hard on my scrawling, so I knew that my attention to detail towards making every letter a piece of perfect script made my application all the better.

It was a work of art.

I read and re-read the rules, each time feeling that nothing had ever fit me so perfectly in all my life. Then, after postmarking it and proofreading the mailing address three times, I'd walked the envelope down Main Street to the faded, rusting blue post office box bolted to the sidewalk in front of my dad's shop and dropped it inside with a single blessing.

Please.

The events that followed my submission of that application included notification of my status as a finalist and subsequent summer evenings spent emailing the nine other 4-H members who found themselves in the same position. We got to know one as much as a few misspelled sentences in an email can allow, sharing our fears about the upcoming interview with the panel of judges and talking about our equine projects for our individual county fairs in the summer of 2004. The more I talked to other finalists, the more I knew I wouldn't be the one taking the award horse home.

Her name was Belle, they'd told us. The coordinators of the award had emailed us updates, and told us the horse they'd secured for the award was a bay filly registered as *Am I Perfect For You*. They called her "Belle" around the barn.

All ten of us thought she was perfect for us.

Most of them had more experience than I did. Most of them lived on farms and had multiple horses in their family and had parents who rode, showed, or trained horses. I lived just off Main Street in a town on one had ever heard of, borrowed all of the horses I ever showed, and would have no option but to board the horse if I won her.

I didn't have a chance.

On the day of the final judging, I left my interview couldn't recount any of my questions or answers until I was on the midway with a famous Dairy Barn shake. Then, I could barely remember glimpses of my performance, from being called to enter the room with the judges, to stepping into the long, dark room, to having to walk in silence several yards to my seat.

I sat, folding my hands in my lap, awaiting my fate.

"Why do you want this horse?" the first question fired.

"Because... I want her."

It was all I could recall from any of the questions or answers that must have transpired in the subsequent twenty minutes. So, after a recess on the midway, I returned to the arena for the award ceremony, perfectly convinced that I had come in last place.

I listened as the runner-up was announced, and it wasn't me. I'm not sure where my conscious went, but I wasn't present in the arena any longer, drifting instead into some daydream as I often did.

The video that my mom took from the side of the arena shows an awkward silence among the remaining nine contestants who weren't named as the runner-up. No one stood when the winner of the horse was announced.

I can only imagine that, after the final announcement, I must have calculated that if no one else was moving, it must have been my name that was called. I don't have any recollection of hearing my own name vibrating off the speakers, nor of standing to accept the prize. The first memory I have inside the arena is of walking towards an excitable filly as a grinning man extended the lead rope towards one of my hands, shaking the other in congratulations.

Belle.

A fourteen-year-old memory that grew sweeter with time.

She was fifteen years old on our anniversary in 2018, the same age I'd been when I took her home. She had become a more amiable partner with every year.

I couldn't imagine a more perfect role model to help Noel settle into society.

Joe had come out to the barn to present Belle with her anniversary bouquet of carrots. I rarely had a few hours of his time undivided by Army obligations, so I wanted to take advantage of the extra set hands while I had them at my disposal.

I didn't have a trailer of my own in 2018, but I had arranged for a roomy, four-horse trailer to stay parked in the arena for several days so that we could practice loading on and off of it.

My strategy was painfully detailed, accounting for multiple contingencies and every possible way that Noel could react. Having learned that her behaviors were never predictable in a traditional sense, I hoped that if I planned for twelve different possible reactions, surely I'd come close with one of them.

"Noel has never gotten on a trailer and gotten back off the trailer at the same place," I explained to defend the complexity of my strategy. "This is probably going to bring back some unpleasant memories, and Noel may even panic."

I couldn't imagine the experience, stepping foot on her first trailer at two weeks of age and leaving California forever. She'd stood on a bouncing, bumbling trailer for more hours in her lifetime than some people spend, cumulatively, at the gym. California, to Utah, to three different places in Colorado. Now, as she had spent less than a year at her newest home, I was preparing to ask her to step onto a dark, enclosed trailer again.

"My goal is one hoof," I stated aloud, setting my intentions. One hoof inside the trailer, and then we could end the session. If I could just show her that putting some part of her body inside the trailer would be safe, rewarded with cookies, and that she'd go back to her comfortable house with Belle, perhaps she'd mull it over, donkey-style, and be less scared the next time I asked her to approach a trailer.

We headed out to the arena with Joe leading Belle, and I breathed a little easier only having one animal to manage. I knew when I started seeking a Forever Friend that the rest of my walks with Belle would be forever altered by having to manage two animals at the end of two separate ropes, but it was the right choice at the time, and it continued to work well. It was a sacrifice worth making.

Joe let the girls graze along the fence line for a few minutes while I prepared the trailer. I opened both of the rear doors and tied them in place with ropes so that they wouldn't slam and startle Noel. I cleared the interior of the trailer, removing the few items that were stored inside. I opened the front windows to allow as much light as possible into the small space.

Then, pulling Belle's head away from the grass, Joe led her to the back of the trailer and she immediately, calmly stepped aboard- the exact same way she'd been so willing to jump aboard the trailer to go home with us after the award presentation at the Indiana State Fair exactly fourteen years prior. The only difference was that Belle had matured physically and packed a few hundred more pounds onto her stout frame.

"Okay, we're up." Both my poker face and voice had improved over the two-thirds of a year that I'd been practicing how to better communicate with the burro on my right side.

Belle whinnied from inside the trailer, making sure that Noel was still nearby even though she was temporarily out of sight. Noel characteristically stayed quiet, but she was aware that her big sister was looking for her, and she walked willingly towards the back of the trailer.

Joe stood at the front of the trailer with Belle, depositing snacks in her mouth at a steady pace. I smiled seeing Belle in her happiest emotional state of being- standing still and eating food.

Noel stopped when we got to the back of the trailer and swished her tail. It was a far less explosive first approach than I'd anticipated, but I was sure it was coming.

I stepped into the trailer first, backing up a few small steps, then turning briefly to gauge Belle's positioning and create some spatial awareness for Noel.

When I turned back around less than a full second later, I was taken aback to see that Noel had silently leapt aboard the trailer in the time I'd averted my gaze from her.

Ears standing tall, Noel was stretching her soft muzzle towards me, expecting the same snacks that Belle was enjoying.

My jaw dropped. I quickly fished a cookie from my pocket- I hadn't even had a reward ready to gift because I was anticipating a lengthy process to get a single hoof inside.

Noel crunched happily, sniffed around the trailer, lifted her head to look out the window, then calmly stepped off the trailer into the sand and went about her day.

I looked back at Joe guiding Belle off the trailer, and shrugged, still in awe, then started laughing.

"Well, I guess I still have no idea what I'm doing."

August 26, 2018
Black Forest, Colorado
Three Years Captive
One Year, Three Months Rescued
Seven Months, Twenty-Three Days Home

For the sake of my sanity, I had traded my day shifts for a night shift schedule once again, and found my body chronically wracked with fatigue. Feeling like I was in a constantly hungover state, the daylight stung my corneas when I ventured outside anytime between dawn and dusk.

Noel was willing to act as my confidant in a way that Belle didn't want to serve, and I told her all about my schedule switch while she leaned into me with her hips, expecting rubs in her favorite place above the base of her tail.

"Imagine the most terrible manager you've ever met, a vile and incompetent woman who 'manages' an inpatient medical floor but can't even turn on an IV pump by herself, who makes decisions about who gets to go on vacation based on how much she likes you as a friend and not on the quality of your work," I vented to Noel as dramatically as I could to emphasize my points.

Her big, brown eyes were soft. It was hard to even remember them being hardened with fear in the spring. She'd likely endured unsavory management at some point in her journey from California, to Utah, to Colorado, to me- the odds mandated it. But she was still willing to lend an ear while I complained about mine, distracting me only when the time was right by backing towards my lap as if she was about to take a seat, like a big dog on hooves.

She swooped her nose towards her knees, shooing a collection of unrelenting black flies away. Their exodus revealed several pinpoint spots of blood from the bites they'd inflicted.

"What are we going to do about those," I half-asked, half-lamented.

Her lips were relaxed into an expression that resembled a jovial smirk, diving again to rid her legs of the flies.

I haven't done the math on how much I'd spent on fly repellent in the summer of 2018, and I have no desire to know how many dollars had gone down the drain. Nothing worked to keep the flies off Noel. They were unshakeable.

I'd invested in vet wrap at the price of more than a dollar per roll, but the self-adhesive bandages were always lying in the dirt by the time I returned to the barn. I'd order sixty-dollar fly boots online. Noel watched me apply them, then just as quickly learned how to undo the Velcro straps that kept them fastened. Despite all the wasted money and weekly trials on new ideas, I hadn't won the fly battle yet.

It would take something that Noel couldn't remove to thwart the flies this season, like a hefty roll of duct tape, or...

"Girl!" I said excitedly. "Hold on, I have an idea."

I jumped up and moved towards the gate quickly, Noel trotting next to me.

"Hold on! I'll be right back."

I shut the gate softly in her face, her look of intrigue following me on my jog towards my car.

I had to turn the radio up as soon as I buckled my seatbelt, as had become my norm, because it made me feel bad to hear her braying after me.

I wish I could have explained in a way she'd understand that I'd be right back.

Dollar Tree, Walmart, and Domino's were essentially the only stores in Falcon, Colorado, though there are few other staples a little town needs. I parked outside the dollar store, ran inside for only a few minutes, then turned the car around with a plastic bag full of options in the seat next to me.

"Noel." I rounded the corner with a pair of socks and scissors, sizing up her legs and making an educated guess on what pair to use. I made a cut across the toe. "Let's put on a pair of socks."

Noel looked at me with as much excitement as she'd had when I presented her with the traffic cone, which, at the time of the sock donning, still sat untouched in the corner of the pen.

Then she stood quietly while I rolled the toeless socks over her hooves and up her legs.

They stayed.

October 1, 2018
Colorado Springs, Colorado
Three Years, Two Months Captive
One Year, Five Months Rescued
Eight Months, Twenty-Eight Days Home

The time stamp on the first document I saved reminded me of the day I had the idea to write a book about gentling a wild burro.

I had books about donkeys on my shelves. How to train, breed, and select donkeys based on conformation, how to start a mule under saddle. But none spoke about burros. None of the training books about donkeys prepared me for how to interact with a wild animal in the early phase of her gentling. None of the resources I'd pored over mentioned the fundamental differences between an animal who had been raised in an environment with more individualized attention, perhaps with a tame dam, rather than the wide open holding facility surrounded by untamed souls.

It's not easy nor ethical to write a book educating the general public when the author herself is not a subject matter expert. But, I realized, the novice does have an advantage in some aspects of learning over the expert.

Experts forget. Professional horse, donkey, and mule trainers are so good at what they do that they forget the little things that aren't second nature to beginners. Experts forget that an amateur horse person who hasn't trained an equine in fifteen years needs a refresher on effectively applying and removing pressure to achieve the proper response. Forget that amateurs have never removed the halter from a timid, untamed animal for the first time. Forget that something second nature for the experienced requires an explanation broken down into twenty smaller steps for someone less experienced.

The amateur is better at finding words to convey information in an easy-to-read format for fellow beginners because they know where their own gaps in knowledge became problematic when they were poring over resources written by the experts.

The best of both worlds, then, is to start drafting as a novice and finish editing as an authority on the subject.

Even as I strived to hone my expertise, I didn't want to forget the facts and tips that hadn't been second nature to me during my first few months with a burro under my care. They were the types of things that likely make long-time donkey enthusiasts say, "I knew that. How does anyone not know that?"

As I constantly learn and improve, they might become things that I look back at in a few years and scoff, "that's not the best way to manage that specific type of behavior." I hope that's the case. But, in the meantime, I also want to remember this phase of newness, of struggling to connect the dots and feeling like I have no idea what I'm doing.

I think a lot of people find themselves in that same position when they get in over their heads with animals who are more difficult to train than they imagined, and I'm sure the fear of being in that position prohibits others from even embarking upon the journey in the first place.

With hundreds and hundreds of unwanted burros in government holding facilities, perhaps a little transparency could shed enough light on an otherwise murky topic that people might feel more empowered to bring their own burro home. Some training books and blogs depict a flawless, linear progression in training, but that's not how life works, especially not when anything long-eared is involved.

So, on the first of October, I started a new document, a place to collect my thoughts, thinking I could share them one day, candidly, without filtering the things that went wrong. When people understand what parts of new burro ownership went off-plan and they can make plans to circumvent the mistakes that I made, maybe more burros, or even mustangs, will find homes.

Fifty thousand burros and mustangs combined sitting in government holding facilities with good homes few and far between.

Knowledge is power.

The journey to find that knowledge is even more powerful.

On October first, I started writing.

October 25, 2018
Colorado Springs, Colorado
Three Years, Two Months Captive
One Year, Five Months Rescued
Nine Months, Twenty-Two Days Home

Just one day without a scheduled shift to recover.
Ugh.

I left a twelve hour night shift at 7:15 A.M. on a Wednesday, slept all day, slept a little more Wednesday night, and had to return to work at 8:00 A.M. on Thursday to run a pediatric health conference I had organized to provide continuing education to my peers.

I was already unmotivated to follow through with the event. Despite the evidence-based practice I'd found to improve the care of our pediatric patients, all of my ideas had been squashed by others at the hospital, and then one had adopted my project as her own, carrying it to fruition in a manner barely resembling my original vision.

I should have learned over the past year and a half that it's not worth having original ideas in an outdated facility that refuses to join the rest of the world of health care, but my drive to improve continued to overtake my discouragement over every one of my ideas that had been either stolen by an incompetent manager who could not come up with her own ideas.

I just had to complete one last obligation that I'd worked hard to bring to reality. I just had to implement this one final event that had been in the works for months, started before the hospital had completely broken me. Then I'd be on my way to Denver to catch a flight to California, and I could spend four wonderful days at the annual Donkey Welfare Symposium that I'd signed up to attend at the University of California in Davis, absorbing all the information about donkeys that I could fit into my brain.

I arrived early at the hospital to set up, tackle last minute problems, communicate with conference attendees, meet the speakers, and provide a quick tour of the facility. I then became a participant at the pediatric health care conference that I had organized myself, learned new evidence-based practice, honed skills to more effectively provide lifesaving interventions for our youngest clientele, and helped clean up after the event.

A long day in if its own, concluded with a long drive north.

It pained me to cruise by the exit that would have taken my car to the barn. I missed my girls, and I wouldn't see them for four more days. But I was confident that the new information I was bound to acquire at U.C. Davis would benefit my donkmanship and ultimately be good for Noel.

My brain was tired. Two conferences in two days, each a stark juxtaposition of the other. The first, I'd been dreading, but the second, I couldn't wait to start.

Everything was packed into a carry-on bag to save both time and money. I was already going to be landing in Sacramento after 10:00 P.M., so I had no desire to spend any more time loafing around a baggage carousel. Plus, the four-day trip had already racked up a tab of over a thousand dollars between flights and a hotel room, so I planned on pinching pennies during the rest of my stay. I wasn't even planning on eating out. I had packed granola bars that I'd gotten on sale at the grocery store and I was going to be raid the free continental breakfast at the hotel for bagels and coffee on my way to the symposium.

I caught an Uber at the airport that took me to my hotel, which was not far away. It was my first time flying to a new part of the country on my own. And, as weary as I was, it was exciting to have figured out all the steps without anyone else's help.

I had a heightened sense of awareness, arriving at the hotel so late at night. I checked in at the front desk and then walked outside to my motel room, disappointed to find a door that faced the exterior of the building- the easiest kind of room for murderers to infiltrate.

Pushing an armchair up against the door, I left the lamp on and had no problem drifting happily to sleep.

The sooner I fell asleep, the sooner morning would arrive.

October 26, 2018
Davis, California
Three Years, Two Months Captive
One Year, Five Months Rescued
Nine Months, Twenty-Two Days Home

    In stark contrast to the day before, I arrived excitedly a full hour before the first presentation was set to start. I craved the knowledge I was about to soak in, and I couldn't wait to get started.

    And learn I did. The speakers garnered my attention, and I filled page after page in a notebook with all my new knowledge and ideas I wanted to implement.

    I hadn't even made it through half a day away from the hospital when I got a phone call from a familiar number. Ugh. I silenced my phone to ignore the call. We were in the middle of a lecture, and I was not about to leave one of my classes to deal with headaches from work. So, dreading what the conversation was going to be about, I waited until my lunch break and then called the number back.

    "Is there a reason that you reported at eight hours of work yesterday on your time card when you did not work for eight hours?" the angry voice of a member of my chain of command barked over the telephone.

    "Excuse me?!" I was taken aback, and rightfully so, recalling the amount of work and time in excess of eight hours that I had spent organizing and attending the event.

It shouldn't have warranted a reply. I should have reminded my manager that I had cashed in hours of leave to take a break from work just to get away from that particular kind of stress and idiocrasy. I should have responded even more incredulously at the accusation that was being brought against me. I shouldn't have called the number back at all, actually, knowing before that call even connected that it was just going to ruin my day.

I exhibited far too much restraint, a habit which likely contributed to my burnout in the position. But, I politely explained that I had arrived to work at 8:00 A.M. and then listed all of the tasks that I had completed. Brainstorming ways to prove the words that I was saying, I suggested that my manager go speak to this person and that person that I had greeted when I arrived at the hospital early in the morning. I remembered having sent an email shortly after I arrived, and I knew it would have a time stamp to serve as another piece of evidence to prove my case.

It was frustrating that I was in a position to have to prove the words that I was saying. It should have been another nail in the coffin to prompt me to write a resignation letter. But, in the name of my paycheck, I persisted.

It's unfortunate that thoughts of work still mar the memories of the events that I experienced that weekend. I dived even deeper into the curriculum, trying to escape from the other stressors in my life a thousand miles east of my seat on the bleachers outside the arena in the California sun.

As soon as we had our next break, I pulled up a job search on my phone. *People don't leave jobs*, I remember hearing from a former coworker who had vacated her position at the hospital. *They leave managers.*

I was understanding more and more how true that was. I liked the responsibilities of my job, liked the patient population that I cared for, but it made me sick to my stomach to be working for this type of management.

Good managers are few and far between. I'd had a good boss before, but it was hard to appreciate at the time. It had easily been ten years since I'd worked under a good manager, at a manufacturing plant, of all places. I hadn't realized how lucky I was to be working for that individual until I had to experience working for multiple corrupt and lazy managers.

I wasn't even supposed to have the manufacturing job originally. I'd heard a knock on our front door, and I opened it to greet the man who produced aviation hardware manufacturing equipment a couple blocks from our house. He was looking for my younger brother to offer him some hours working in the shop.

But my brother was busy with other work, and I wasn't, so I had offered up my own two hands instead. The man that took me up on my offer, and I started operating a punch press stamping unique pieces of hardware to be used in airplane manufacturing.

Never having bought into traditional gender roles, it didn't feel that foreign to me at the time to be a young female working in a manufacturing plant. It was mundane, monotonous work. The same repetitive motion every three or four seconds for the entirety of a work day. It wasn't bad work, though, and it wasn't significant manual labor. Just boring.

The nature of the work combined with me being a teenager at the time, plus the luxury of living two blocks from work resulted in me showing up a few minutes later each day, simply because I could. It wasn't a big deal, seemingly to me at the time. I wasn't clocking into a machine, and I still got my work done. At the time, I didn't understand the significance of showing up at 8:10 A.M. when I was scheduled to arrive at 8:00.

The boss who had hired me, the owner of the company, came to my house one morning at 8:05 when I had been scheduled to show up at 8:00. Still thinking it wasn't a big deal, I was surprised to find the man genuinely concerned. He asked if I had been treated okay in the shop. I assured him that I had, but his concerned expression didn't fade. He pressed on, wanting to make sure I had felt welcome, that I understood the job, and that there was no extenuating circumstance causing me to show up late.

I felt bad. I hadn't meant to worry him. Now, a decade after the fact, I still remember the effort he took to get to the bottom of the reason behind my behavior. It takes a strong leader to care that much about a temporary employee. Now, having worked under quite a few poor leaders, I realized that I hadn't fully appreciated the opportunity I'd been given to learn from a good boss.

I got bitter again thinking back to that memory. Being accused of time fraud from a thousand miles away when I put in nothing but hour after hour of unappreciated work was sickening. I wanted out. And because I was in a place surrounded by donkeys that needed training, trainers wanting to impart their wisdom, and a crowd of people who wanted to better at themselves for the sake of the animals, the train of thought in my head started to gravitate towards the animals I was watching before me in the arena. A wild burro resembling Noel was trying to get away from the trainer on the end of the rope.

I scoffed under my breath because I understood what the animal must be thinking.

Trying to get away in a physical sense, the way I was trying to get away in an emotional and mental capacity.

We were the same.

If the parallels between myself as an employee and a burro as a newly-captive animal translate so well, could the same parallels be made between a manager and a handler?

Yes, it made perfect sense.

A good manager is a leader.

A good animal handler is a leader.

I continued to connect the dots. If I sought a manager who cared to know not just about what behaviors I was exhibiting, but also why, then surely the same is true of an animal who is looking to a human for leadership.

All animals innately exhibit behavior- every reaction, every move an animal makes is behavior, by definition. And every behavior has at least one motivating factor. Some motivating factors are positive, like migrating in the wild to find food or shelter. Some behaviors are negative, like fleeing from a person out of fear of injury or punishment. But there is always a factor of some sort driving the action that an animal exhibits.

As a good leader, why was I not spending more time seeking to more completely understand the *why* rather than judging the reaction at face value?

I needed to be a better leader.

It would have been nice to have a role model at work to help shape my ability to lead, but instead I'd have to draw on decade-old memories and come up with the rest from scratch.

November 20, 2018
Black Forest, Colorado
Three Years, Three Months Captive
One Year, Six Months Rescued
Ten Months, Seventeen Days Home

"I know, my girl, and I'm sorry, but it's only a week."

I wrapped my arms around her neck from my old seat on the overturned bucket and Noel curled her head around mine. A burro hug, the warmest kind of embrace.

Exactly a year ago, I had laid eyes upon her for the first time. Twelve short months later, it was hard to leave her behind for a week at a time.

But, I'd learned my lesson. Terry taught me that it's never okay to put family on the back burner.

Animals are important. Work is important. Family is irreplaceable.

But I still felt bad.

Desperate times called for extra cookies.

"Do you even remember where you were a year ago?"

The question was more for my sake than hers. Of course she remembered. Burros never forget, not anything, not ever.

I remembered, too.

From untouchable to craving human connection.

Brown eyes that had been hollow, now soft and curious.

From timid to the loudest voice on the ranch.

Body language that had been reserved, now bold and authoritative.

From fearful to empowered.

Once cowering alone in a corner of her pen, now standing confidently in the way of all who entered.

#0433 to Zorba to Noel.

From captive to domestic.

November 27, 2018
Black Forest, Colorado
Three Years, Three Months Captive
One Year, Six Months Rescued
Ten Months, Twenty-Four Days Home

Noel was upset.

"Hi, girls." I had announced my presence as I walked around the corner of the barn to greet them after a week away. Breathing deeply the scent of hay and horses, I was happy to be back. I routinely missed out on seeing them for three days in a row when I worked back-to-back-to-back twelve-hour shifts at the hospital, but a seven day stretch was harder to spend away.

Living at a very nice horse stable nestled between groves of tall pines, Belle and Noel always got the best care in terms of food, water, and a clean pen, so there was no need to worry about them from a fundamental perspective. I always felt bad, though, when my extended absence deprived them of turnout time in the big, grassy field, and even more so, I missed being with them. Spending any amount of time in the barnyard offered a level of peace and contentment unparalleled to anywhere else I've been able to find, despite how much I loved living in the shadow of Pike's Peak.

As I hopped around freshly-poured puddles making my way towards their pen, Noel's long ears initially flicked into an alert position, eyeing me through the fence. I was surprised that my return didn't earn me a loud bray, as it usually did when I'd been away for awhile. Belle lifted her head from the pile of hay at her knees, her much shorter ears pricked forward, and nickered at me, expecting cookies. Of course, I had arrived prepared with a pocketful. I unclipped the chain from around the gate to let myself into their pen.

Belle pranced towards me, nose first, on a mission to discover where her snacks were stashed today. But Noel stood back. Usually pushing her way past Belle to be the first to welcome me to their house, she worked to keep some distance between us today.

I scratched Belle's itchy spots under her mane and on her chest, and she tilted her muzzle towards the sky, twitching her lips in a display of satisfaction. Noel, usually pressing up against me while she waited for her own scratches, watched from the corner of her eye with a disgruntled expression.

"What's up, girl," I inquired, taking a step closer to her.

Noel took one step away from me and stopped.

"Are you okay, girl?"

I reached my arm towards Noel's neck and she took one more step away, stopping decisively and tipping her head towards me just slightly enough that I could see her lower an upper eyelid when she looked at me.

I recognized that look.

Noel was upset with me, the way friends become irritated with each other when one feels that the other is ignoring her.

"I'm sorry I was away," I apologized, absentmindedly moving towards her again.

For a third time, Noel scooted just as far away from me as I moved towards her.

"Okay, okay, I get it."

I placed a cookie in the palm of my hand for Belle, who snatched it with her lips as soon as I presented it to her. Then, although suspecting I already knew the outcome, I stretched a cookie in my fingertips towards Noel.

She turned her nose away, her eyelid still lowered enough to make it clear that she was glaring at me, and sauntered away to graze for stray bits of hay on the opposite side of the paddock.

Too upset for cookies. That is a significant level of anger for a donkey who is always hungry.

Okay. I'd give her a few minutes to warm back up to me.

I overturned a plastic barrel to create my familiar seat about fifteen feet away from Noel's pile of hay, waiting for her to grow bored of giving me the cold shoulder and come over for her share of the cookies. The usually-sporadic cell service was nonexistent, and I hadn't brought anything to read or even a notebook for doodling. So, after Belle returned to munching on her dinner, there wasn't much to do other than sit with my own thoughts.

I rolled up my pant legs to soak in the sunshine on my shins, and sat, baking and thinking, waiting for my donkey to forgive me. I wondered how many other people have to apologize to their pets after they come home from vacation.

Apologizing to an animal is a difficult task. How, exactly, can one convey an apology to a creature that doesn't speak English? The words, "I'm sorry," are easy to say to someone who knows what they mean. And, even when those words ring hollow, sharing a common spoken language allows people to explain the reasons behind the actions that hurt their friend.

"I went on a trip with my family," I explained to Noel from my seat on the barrel, knowing that even though Noel couldn't understand the words, my tone of voice conveyed meaning as well.

Angled away from me, Noel kept her rump squarely between me and her line of sight. When I spoke, she lifted her head slightly and turned it enough to glare at me again from the corner of her eye, snorting curtly in my direction.

I sighed and let silence again fall over us. I had only planned a quick trip to the barn tonight. I still needed to unpack my suitcase and stop at the grocery store to restock the fridge. I wondered for a moment if I should just let Noel finish her dinner in solitude and try again tomorrow. No, I decided. I wasn't sure yet what was going to remedy my newly-strained relationship with my donkey, but I was fairly confident that leaving her again would only turn the knife in the emotional wound I had created by abandoning Noel to go on a lengthy trip.

Sitting alone in the quiet barnyard allowed me to get lost in my thoughts. Meditation. It began to occur to me that true friends, mature friends, don't get upset when their pals go on vacations, or spend some time on their own for a brief while. On the human spectrum, the kind of friends who get upset when other people have fun without them tend to be self-centered, a little dramatic, or even catty.

You can't personify animals. The sudden memory popped up, derailing my train of thought and taking me briefly back to the Donkey Symposium in California.

It's interesting that some of the quotes that stuck with me the most were the things with which I disagreed. I distinctly remember a graduate student who was studying donkey behavior stand to speak, and half-joking that her professor admonished her for anthropomorphizing some of her subjects. "Of course, you can't personify donkeys," she said at a dinner event one evening.

But I disagreed then and even considerable reflection on the topic didn't change my mind. The concept lingered in the back of my mind here and there when I worked with Noel. Personifying Noel's behaviors and reactions helped me understand her better. In fact, the more I thought about it, the more I thought that it would be an injustice to Noel to fail to personify her. She has emotions that mirror humans in many ways, from fear, to joy, to anger. In many cases, the events that spark those emotions are human-like, too. A threat to safety triggers her to experience fear, and the first warm, sunny day after a streak of rain sparks joy and contentment. Thinking of Noel's behaviors in a humanistic way help explain why she reacts certain ways, and helps me think critically about how to interact with her. Without words.

Because, I've never spoken English to communicate with Noel. I felt stupid immediately. Had a week away from the barn really caused me to forget how to interact with my donkey and help us solve problems together? All things considered, Noel's unhappy mood upon my return to the barn was one of the smallest obstacles we've experienced during our year-long partnership. When she had moved her body away from me to prevent me from making physical contact, it was out of deliberate choice, her attempt to communicate with me. It wasn't out of fear, the way it had been just over a year ago when it took all the courage she could muster just to let me sit as close to her as I was now, upon my bucket.

Now a fully domesticated donkey, I could personify Noel more accurately than ever before. We truly had formed a *partnership*, I realized, as I thought of her progression over the past several months. The more I mulled it over, the more I concluded that it was necessary to think of us as both partners and friends rather than as master-and-pet-donkey. Noel was not my pet. It was not only unfair but also inaccurate to think of her as "my" donkey, as being the "master" of a creature implies having some level of control. She wasn't my pet, or anyone else's. There are few things any human can force a donkey to do, or to not do. While it's my choice to confine her to a pen at a stable, having any control over her actions within the pen is another concept entirely. When she responds positively, it's because she chooses to play along. When I ask her for a specific action because she respects me as a team member, not because I'm mandating any specific response. I earned her respect over time by respecting her first. To earn her trust, I first had to trust her- no small task, at times. After spending so much time together, we had developed a mutual understanding as partners. We were friends with the contingency that neither of us would disrespect the partnership. And my absence had upset the balance.

I circled back to the railcar on my train of thought that I'd been pondering before getting sidetracked. Mature friends don't get upset over a few days without one-on-one attention, but self-centered friends do.

But Belle had been in my life for fourteen years longer than Noel, and Belle hadn't been catty upon my return. Rather, she behaved the opposite, greeting me excitedly because she knew I'd have extra cookies to make up for my absence. She was always happy to see me.

She was always easy to direct, willing to go with the flow, never stopping to demand that she get her own way. When she was upset, she got over it quickly. Always mellow, never reacting too dramatically to any event or situation. We were still partners- it's hard to mandate the actions of a half-ton creature without having some level of mutual respect- but it seemed to be more understood that I was the leader. In situations that startled Belle, she was quicker to seek my guidance, whereas her long-eared counterpart insisted on analyzing the situation herself and coming to her own conclusions.

If I labeled Belle as a person, she would be the come-over-anytime-for-a-pitcher-of-sangria-and-casual-conversation best friend who gets along with everyone. Sweet Belle, gently flicking her tail side to side as she methodically sorted through her pile of hay. Bringing home a burro had changed my perspective of horse ownership, and made the albeit-larger animals with short ears seem so much easier to manage.

I took advantage of my time to think by ruminating over the ranks of the equine in a societal hierarchy. If Belle was the reliable, easygoing, neighborly friend, then that would make Noel the equivalent of her sassy, teenage daughter, I mused, observing the shaggy steadfast creature in front of me who continued to ignore my presence.

The more I pondered the traits that Noel shared with a stereotypical teenage drama queen, the more the persona fit. Even with our mutual trust and respect at this stage of our partnership, Noel still naturally tended to react dramatically, and kept people laughing with her expressive face. Especially considering the glare that peeked out from under the pile of gray fuzz on her forehead, it was hard to deny that Noel as a person would likely be the strong-willed, loud-mouthed leader of a clique in a PG-13 movie set in a high school.

I humored the idea, transitioning from the romanticized idea of our partnership to the more lighthearted perspective of the way Noel's current attitude would fit into the cast of *Mean Girls*.

If Noel is a sassy teenager who's holding a grudge, I realized, *I'm just adding fuel to her fire by trying so desperately to get back in her good graces.*

So, how do you earn the attention of a sassy drama queen who's trying to prove a point by ignoring you...

I crossed my arms and rotated my body away from Noel, removing my attention from her. The sun was fading, and I rolled my pants back down to cover my legs. It was the most perfect time of evening, when I can retire my sunglasses to the top of my head without needing to squint and enjoy the golden cast of retreating light washing over one of my favorite places in Colorado.

Belle and Noel's pen sat squarely in the middle of the peaceful barnyard. On the north side of their pen was the main barn, buttoned up tightly for the night, a dozen horses inside chewing happily on dwindling racks of hay. On the east, the best-travelled aisleway in the barnyard afforded the opportunity to greet and interact with lots of human and equine passers-by. It had been a source of stress for Noel upon her arrival to the barn as a nearly-untouchable burro, but now it was a source of intrigue as she'd learned that she often got handouts and scratches from the visitors who walked past her pen. On the south side, a series of additional pens housed beautiful animals who Belle and Noel had gotten to know as harmless acquaintances. And on the west, their closest neighbor, Elvis, took up residence, the only other horse that shared a fence line with the girls. He was looking at me, I saw, under the guise of taking a sip of water from their shared tank. He knew I spared an occasional handout and was always good for a nose rub.

Even having diverted all my attention elsewhere to gaze around, Noel refused to take notice. So, testing my new theory, I got up and walked towards Elvis. Turning to look at Noel, I saw her face still buried in her hay, but a watchful eye now fixated on me.

"Hi, Elvis," I gushed, scratching him between his eyes. He stretched his nose through the fence, his nostrils flaring. It's rarely easy to keep a pocketful of cookies a secret in a crowded barnyard.

I continued to shower him with attention. "Oh, are you a good boy?" I cooed, offering a cookie. He took it from my hand and crunched it loudly.

I had never been able to gauge Noel's movements by sound. A trait that must have evolved from her predecessors' time spent living in the wilds of southern California, Noel was able to move completely silently, even at a brisk pace. I had to turn partially around to see that Noel had left the remains of her dinner when I started giving her cookies away to other, more grateful, souls.

She still stood more than an arm's length away, but for the first time since my arrival, Noel faced me squarely with her ears pointed towards me.

"Hi, girl," I said again, for the first time since my initial attempt to greet her an hour earlier.

She didn't move her feet, but stretched her neck to move her nose closer to me.

"You want to be my friend again now?"

I extended a cookie towards her. A peace offering.

She took it without hesitation this time, chewing thoughtfully. She had always plucked treats from my hands so gently, and always spent triple the time anyone else did chewing it and enjoying the moment.

I thought about stepping towards her to scratch her jaw in her itchiest spot, but forced myself to refrain and reformulate my body language around my new theory. If Noel and I were currently engaged in the equivalent of a high-school-best-friends-spat, it wouldn't be over with a single olive branch. Sixteen-year-old human girl grudges always outlast one hour and a cookie.

I turned back away from Noel to give Elvis one more pat, then I walked away, past Noel, back to my barrel. I sat down facing away from both Noel and her hay.

Again, she was silent. Even straining to hear the smallest clue that Noel had perhaps followed me, I had to turn around to see if it was true. It was. Still out of reach, but obviously interested in my new tactic, I had won her attention back.

"Oh, hello, Noel." I acknowledged again, actively looking just past Noel, purposefully refusing to focus my attention back on her yet. Unfortunately, I hadn't been good at the social nuances of high school even when I actually was a sixteen-year-old girl. Always content to spend time away from the crowd, I don't remember ever engaging in the games that seem to accompany dramatic high school friendships and relationships. I had no idea that I would have been preparing to repair a relationship with a disgruntled donkey one day, or I would have been much more motivated to take part. Instead, I had to rely on the behaviors I had quietly observed from the back corner of the classes I'd sat through for four years.

A few moments seemed like eternity as I wondered if I was winning the waltz that I wasn't even fully convinced we were dancing. I tried to keep a poker face as I ignored Noel. The longer I sat on the barrel, staring into space at nothing, the more I wondered if I was, perhaps, crazy.

Curiosity finally got the better of Noel. She took a big step forward, her nose again gravitating towards me, and I rewarded her effort with another bite. More quiet, thoughtful chewing, and, it seemed, we were friends again. Tentatively.

It took the better part of an hour, but I finally got to pet Noel's soft summer coat, which had shed out more in the time that I'd been gone. I scratched her jaw and the top of her neck along her mohawk of a mane. Her drooping lower lip suggested that she was at ease, and her eyelids had relaxed to erase any inkling that a cold glare had ever dominated her soft brown eyes. I was forgiven, if at least partially.

I scratched Noel for a few more minutes, then chose to leave on a good note while it was my choice. I drove home content, shifting sequentially through the gears, the radio playing quietly in the background, mulling over the two perspectives I'd explored. I wanted the romanticized concept of my partnership with Noel to trump as the more accurate premise, but realizing I'd gotten better feedback from applying the principles that govern high school in-crowds.

Shaking my head, I reminded myself that understanding donkeys will never be straightforward, nor will I ever be able to describe Noel with a single word.

She's both. Both my revered partner, and my dramatic, teenaged best friend.

And she's even more than that on any given night, and sometimes completely the opposite.

It might have made our journey advance more smoothly if I'd known a year ago what I now understood.

A year since I'd opened my life up to a donkey, and I understood that I would never understand, and that there are no words available in the English language to quantify how donkeys behave, learn, or respond, let alone how human should interact with them.

At least I could be certain of a few things:

Burros don't advance in a linear timeline.

I will never be able to tell a donkey what to do.

Some questions will never have answers.

There's no way for new donkey owners to avoid starting from scratch and learning everything the hard way, because there is no easy way.

Eventually, though, with commitment and desire, a donkey can become both a revered partner, and a sassy best friend.

It hadn't been an easy journey for me, but Noel had the most inconceivably difficult journey of all.

A journey more than three years in the making, with a lifetime yet to go.

Epilogue

Our time in Colorado was undeniably the most magical season in my life thus far.

At the time of publishing, my residency in Colorado is growing to a close. Joe and I are packing, and soon we'll be sleeping under a roof 1,600 miles from the front range I fell in love with the first moment I laid eyes on the Rocky Mountains.

Life in Colorado gave me never-ending gifts. Mountain views that changed by the hour. Fresh, albeit thin, air in my lungs during hikes and long runs. Countless hours enjoyed at the most peaceful ranch east of the Rockies. And Noel.

Reminiscence is more than just remembering. The right mindset and a distance from distracting constraints are necessary to properly reflect upon what happened, what went right, and what could be improved.

If I had a do-over for my three and a half years spent in Colorado, it's hard to say whether I would change anything drastic because I am so satisfied with the status of my endeavors as they sit on my way out. I will always regret not having more time to spend in the shadows of Pike's Peak, and I will always feel like more days could have been spent in the backwoods wilderness and its indescribable beauty.

I left my job a few months before we drove east out of Colorado for the last time. As much as I wanted to quit for the last significant stretch of time in Colorado, it's not easy to say whether that would have been the right choice. The financial freedom allowed by the position facilitated above-adequate care for my animals and set me up to take a few months off work during the interstate move. A job in a different hospital would have allowed more time off work, but would not have paid nearly as well.

However, the size of the salary is certainly not a factor at the top of my list anymore when job seeking. After I'd been away from my former position for a few weeks, I got an email from a credit card company whose card I used to carry. According to the auto-generated email, the company missed my business, wanted me back, and was willing to offer a special rate just to see me return. It hit me that my former credit card company appreciated me more than a job where I'd slaved a minimum of forty hours a week to doing my best work for the most uncaring of managers. Having been so jaded by a corrupt chain of management, I know now I'll never again stoop to gaining employment from someone who looked me in the eye on my last day of employment and failed to even say "thanks" for the hours upon hours of selfless service I'd provided.

There's no way to go back in time and tell whether that would have actually increased my happiness, creativity, and level of productivity in the way that I think it would have.

Similarly, there's no way to tell whether Noel's progress or outcome would have differed at all if I had known along the way what I know now. I do feel infinitely better equipped to help another wild burro in the future navigate the world, but I'm not sure how different Noel would be if I had attempted to train her any differently. I'm pretty proud of her present-day status and the level of our partnership. I feel like I can trust her more completely than I can some of the mature, highly-trained horses at the barn.

Noel is now a donkey, a more civilized version of the wild burro she was when she came home.

And I am now a less civilized, more free-thinking version of my former self.

I think an hour and an overturned bucket can solve more problems than people realize. So, if ever you get the chance to spend time soaking silently in a barnyard, take it.

We'd love to keep in touch!

Follow us on Facebook or Instagram by searching "**Belle and Bray**" and subscribe to **Tess Zorba's Author Page** on Amazon to receive an email when we release new books.

We'd love to read your Amazon review, too, so let us know what you thought of our story!

—Andrea, Belle, and Noel

Made in the USA
Coppell, TX
23 November 2020